MW01268751

AMONG IXORAS

BRYAN KOH

AMONG IXORAS

a collection of recipes from my kitchen in Singapore

PROLOGUE

It has been a strange couple of years to say the least. Some threw themselves into cycling and knitting as a means of coping with uncertainty, others carpentry and yoga. I know many who found immense succour in the company of cats. For me, it was the kitchen that brought distraction and relief. But instead of tinkering with ideas for baked goods and testing recipes furnished by foreign contacts, as are routine, I allowed comfort to be my compass, engaging with the familiar, revisiting dishes to which I lacked access at the time for an assortment of reasons. These ranged from the rice porridges enjoyed by the Teochew side of my family to the *adobo* introduced by my *yaya*, the buttery cakes of kindergarten years to the *gulai* and *kerabu* of which my Penang-born mother is exceedingly fond.

Largely assisted by exchanges with my mother and aunts, friend cooks and former househelpers, I cooked and recorded, tweaked and updated until, one day, I decided to stop. The resultant notebook of recipes was then put away, future retrievals meant solely for personal use, not anything larger. It was only when I began cooking from it for friends at home that the collection seemed to possess ample intrigue, perhaps quirk, to warrant release. So here we are.

The book that eventually wrapped itself around these dishes inadvertantly, though not entirely unexpectedly, became about the past accounting for the present. Our relationship with food during our youth, as well as our connection with its associated spaces, from market to table, has an undeniable influence on our palates and often has a hand in shaping our passions and our attitudes towards life as a whole.

Unlike my previous literary endeavours, built on adventure and fuelled by curiosity and wanderlust, this svelte creature is quite different in its being largely inward-looking. It is not so much a book on Singapore food, rather one about the food that I grew up eating in Singapore. Home food, basically.

Beyond their gastronomic value, it is the memories hovering in the orbit of these dishes, random and trivial, yet critical and profound, that I find just as compelling. A flip through the recipe list dredges up the scent of freshly rendered coconut oil with which the domestics would anoint their manes, the sound of my grandmother scraping char off biscuity tiles of toast, the sight of fellow students at primary school, among ixora shrubs, snapping off vivid corymbs and sucking nectar from stamens.

Given its nature, it seemed apposite to hew *Among Ixoras* as close to my personality as possible. And I have always been more comfortable letting food do the speaking.

FIVE STONES

For me, the mind balloons that appear at the mere mention of "school" have their strings firmly fastened to the years of prepubescence. The monkey bars, rusty from rain. The worn hopscotch markings on black rubber flooring. The smell of chalk boards, the devastating temptation to scratch them. Games of flag erasers and five stones. The transience of mealtimes.

Despite the three-and-a-half decades separating me from the days of pre-school, my memories of kindergarten meals have not been entirely lost. I still remember the jejune bowls of macaroni chicken soups and soy-dimmed rice fried with a frustration of frozen vegetables, while our teachers applied themselves to bowls of rice porridge, a conjoined pair of *you tiao* resting where chopsticks normally would. I would watch their faces lower to greet filled spoons, rising to reveal stinging looks of contentment.

Mealtimes in primary school were markedly better, indicated on timetables with an eye-gladdening "canteen". This meant a few things. Scrolls of *cheong fun*, napped in a sauce like liquid bitumen, speckled with sesame seeds. Nests of rice vermicelli loosened by hot, limpid chicken broths. Plates of rice coloured with a chaos of viands and sauces. Jaundiced, glutinous triangles of *lopes*, cloaked in plastic, a slick of dark syrup wetting their snowy, coconut frocks in parts.

It was during this time that I came to appreciate what some would term "purchase happiness", the idea that in exchange for several pieces of metal and creased bits of paper, some joy could be had. (For a short while, anyway.)

ROTI SUSU

I have a deep fondness for these pull-apart cushions, often sold in school canteens and local bakeries as six-packs, that those who worship at the Temple of Rugged Crust and Tangy Crumb may find uncomfortably close to Poor Taste.

Roti susu means "milk bread", so it should come as no surprise to learn what the chief liquid is here. Some recipes take the title more seriously and use milk powder and condensed milk. This one does not.

Try warming one or two of these in a toaster oven, splitting them, and covering their still-tender interiors with butter and hae bee hiam. The recipe for the latter rests a flip away, on page 17.

MAKES 1 LOAF

for the tanzhong
35g bread flour
175ml water

for the dough
325g bread flour
75g plain flour
2 tsp dry easy-blend yeast
60g caster sugar
1 tsp salt
60ml vegetable oil, plus more for
   lubricating
60ml milk
1 large egg, lightly beaten

for glazing
1 large egg yolk, lightly beaten
1 tbsp melted butter

Begin with the *tanzhong*. Combine the bread flour and water in a small saucepan. Place the saucepan over medium-low heat and cook, whisking, until you get a bubbling, slightly gloopy, paste. Remove from the heat and cool completely.

Combine the bread and plain flours, dry easy-blend yeast, sugar and salt in a freestanding electric mixer fitted with a dough hook. Flick on the machine and let it whir for a minute or so. Add the *tanzhong*, vegetable oil, milk and beaten egg. At a medium-low speed, incorporate the liquid ingredients into the dry, producing a cohesive, moist, dough. Increase the machine's speed to medium and knead the dough for 15-18 minutes, until smooth and elastic, but still a little sticky. It should pass the windowpane test: a knob of dough should easily be stretched between fingers, allowing light to filter through.

Remove the dough from the mixer bowl, fashion it into a ball and lightly lubricate with oil. Return it to the mixer bowl, cover and leave for 1-2 hours or until doubled in size.

Lightly grease a 22cm square baking tin with vegetable oil. Give the dough a punch-down to expel the air within, then divide it into 9 portions. Roll these into balls. The best way is to trap each one under a cupped hand on a lightly oiled work surface and move it in a circular fashion as if frantically operating a computer mouse. Arrange the balls in a 3x3 formation in the prepared tin. Cover and proof for 1 hour or until the buns have doubled in size.

Preheat the oven to 175°C.

Bake the buns on the second highest shelf for 15-18 minutes or until light gold and puffy. Remove the tray from the oven, lightly paint the buns with beaten egg yolk and bake for another 10 minutes.

Anoint the baked buns with melted butter and give them 15 minutes to compose themselves before eating.

HAE BEE HIAM

The array of spices and aromatics in this thrilling relish of pulverised dried shrimp varies from cook to cook. Its personality runs the gamut from dry as floss to moist and threatening to clump; rough to fine; furious, rusty orange to an austere shade of brick. This version is dryish, rubbly and chocolaty in hue.

It is fine fresh from the pan but tastes best a day or so after being made, when the flavours have had the chance to mingle and make merry. Besides shining on buttered bread, it is very good sprinkled on hot rice.

MAKES approx. 200g

125g dried shrimp
75ml vegetable oil
1 lemongrass stalks, tender portion
  only, bruised
1 tbsp caster sugar
½ tsp salt

for the spice paste
6 garlic cloves, peeled
80g shallots, peeled weight, sliced
2 red chillies, deseeded and sliced
12 dried chillies, deseeded and soaked
  (page 218)
1 tsp fermented shrimp paste
  (*belacan*), toasted (page 219)

Soak the dried shrimp in a bowl of water for 5 minutes. Drain thoroughly and pound with a pestle and mortar or whizz in a cosy blender into a coarse floss.

Similar to the dried shrimp, prepare the spice paste by pounding the garlic, shallots, fresh and dried chillies and toasted fermented shrimp paste with a pestle and mortar until fine. Alternatively, blitz them in a cosy blender with a tiny bit of water.

Heat the vegetable oil in a medium saucepan over medium-high heat. Once hot, add the spice paste. Fry for a minute, stirring furiously, then add the lemongrass stalk, caster sugar, salt and pulverised dried shrimp. Reduce the heat to medium-low and continue frying for 15 minutes, or until the red paste has been transformed into airy, dark brown, confetti. Most of the dampness should have been driven out. Remove and discard the spent lemongrass stalk.

Cool the *hae bee hiam* completely and convey it to an airtight container. You may stow this away in a cool, dry place, but I usually offer it to the refrigerator, where it will be in fine care for 2 months.

KARIPAP

There are numerous theories swirling around attempting to explain the origins of this Southeast Asian pastry. Was it based on the English pasty? The Portuguese empanada, perhaps? The Arab sambusek or its likely descendent the Indian samosa? Was it none, several, or all of the above? Does the origin story differ among the various kinds of curry puffs that exist in the region? Nobody knows for sure.

I would, in general, take a fried curry puff over a baked one. I love the pot–bellied, fragrant richness, that its time in hot fat produces. There are two kinds of fried puffs, those with short, buttery shells and those boasting scaly exteriors effected by alternating leafs of water and oil pastries. They both have merit, but here I supply a recipe for the first, as it is the sort I associate with childhood, on personal and perhaps metaphorical levels.

MAKES 8

for the filling
200g deboned chicken thighs, cut
　　into 1½cm pieces
2 tsp light soy sauce
Finely ground white pepper
3 tbsp ghee
150g yellow onions, peeled and chopped
2 garlic cloves, peeled and minced
1 tbsp ground coriander
2 tsp ground fennel
1 tsp ground chillies
1 tsp ground turmeric
½ tsp ground cumin
Pinch of ground cloves
200g potatoes, peeled weight, cut
　　into 1cm dice
¼ tsp salt, plus more to taste
2 tsp caster sugar
1 tsp fish sauce
100ml chicken stock (page 221)
12 curry leaves
1 hardboiled egg, peeled and cut
　　into 8 pieces (page 219)

In a bowl, combine the chicken thigh pieces with the light soy sauce and a pinch of ground white pepper. Cover and leave to marinate in a cool place for 30 minutes.

Heat the ghee in a large saucepan or wok over medium heat. Once hot, add the onions and fry, stirring, until fragrant, gold-tinged and slightly translucent. Add the garlic and fry for a minute, then add the ground coriander, fennel, chillies, turmeric, cumin and cloves. Cook for 1-2 minutes to eliminate any trace of rawness, being ever watchful of the heat, lest the spices burn. Add a spot more ghee if necessary.

Add the marinated chicken, stirring to seal and coat them in the spices. Stir in the potatoes, salt, caster sugar, fish sauce and chicken stock. Reduce the heat, cover and cook until the potatoes are tender, their edges blurred.

Uncover, stir in the curry leaves and simmer for 5-7 minutes to cook off most of the liquid; there should be just enough moisture to lusciously bind the ingredients. Taste and adjust seasoning with salt and finely ground white pepper. Transfer this richly spiced mixture to a bowl and leave to cool completely while you proceed with the pastry.

for the pastry
300g plain flour
¼ tsp baking powder
½ tsp salt
1 tbsp caster sugar
120g cold unsalted butter, cubed
1 small egg yolk, approx. 13g
Approx. 90ml cold water
Peanut oil, for deep-frying

Combine the plain flour, baking powder, salt and caster sugar in a large bowl and mix well. Add the cubed cold butter and rub it in with your fingers to produce a mess of pale yellow crumbs.

In a small bowl, mix 2 tbsp of the cold water into the egg yolk and stir this into the crumbs. Once this golden liquid has been absorbed, gradually add the remaining cold water, mixing it in to obtain a smooth, cohesive dough, with enough elasticity to allow crimping. Cover and rest for 30 minutes.

On a cool, lightly floured, work surface, divide the dough into 8 portions. Roll these portions into 12cm discs and cover them with a tea towel to prevent them from drying out.

Take one disc of pastry and rest it on a lightly cupped palm. Pile 2 tbsp of the curried filling onto its middle. Use a spoon to flatten the filling slightly and rest a piece of hardboiled egg on top. Now bring both sides of the pastry over the filling so they meet, then pinch them together, expelling as much air as possible, to form a sealed parcel shaped like a half-moon, with a 1cm-wide-lip around its bump. Pinch one of its pointed ends, fold it over and press it down. Continue this pinch-fold-pressing movement, thereby transforming the smooth lip into a crimped spine. Make the rest of the *karipap* this way. (Any leftover filling may be piled onto thick, buttered toast.)

Heat 4cm of peanut oil in a large, deep saucepan or wok over medium heat. Once hot, approximately 175°C, fry the *karipap* in batches until light gold, about 3-4 minutes, pushing them around gently to prevent prolonged contact with the hot metal.

Drain them on kitchen towel and leave to cool slightly before eating.

CHWEE KUEH 水粿

Chwee kueh is a Teochew delicacy, the name meaning "water cake" or "water snack", as they usually emerge from the steamer with a shallow pond of water dampening their faces. That said, the prominence, or indeed presence, of this feature depends on the kind of rice flour and batter-making method used. What is important is that the kueh itself is quivering, slightly clammy, as if courting a nervous breakdown, and almost melt-in-the-mouth, qualities that their traditional coffee-toned clay vessels promote. These have become rare so I, along with most chwee kueh vendors, contend with less romantic metal moulds instead. The ones used in this recipe are 60ml capacity.

You may use either salty or sweet chai poh (preserved radish) for the crucial relish, both of which require a brief soaking period to mellow. I prefer the latter. Some add sesame seeds but I steer clear. The same applies to palate-reddening daubs of sambal, livid with chilli and, quite often, dried shrimp. Do as you feel fit.

MAKES 12

for the batter
100g rice flour
1 tsp tapioca starch
1½ tsp wheat starch
1 tsp salt
300ml water, plus more
350ml boiling water
2 tsp vegetable oil

for the topping
125g sweet chai poh (see above)
4 tbsp lard or vegetable oil
2 garlic cloves, peeled and minced
½ tsp light soy sauce

Combine the rice flour, tapioca and wheat starches and salt in a large measuring jug. Whisk in 150ml of the regular water, followed by the boiling water and oil, until smooth.

Pour 125g of this rice batter into a small saucepan. Into this, add the remaining 150ml regular water and cook over medium-low heat into a soft, spoon-coating paste, whisking constantly. Turn off the heat and scrape this paste into the rest of the batter in the jug. Whisk until smooth, then add enough water to reach the 700ml mark. Cover and set aside for 30 minutes. Meanwhile, prepare your steamer and arrange the moulds (see above) in its perforated tray.

When the water in the steamer is boiling, fill the cups to their brims with the rice batter. Place the tray on the steamer and cover. Steam over high heat for 20 minutes. Remove from the heat and allow the rice cakes to cool completely before unmoulding and arranging on a serving platter.

Meanwhile, make the topping. Wash the *chai poh* 1-2 times to remove surfeit salt and sugar, allowing it to sit in the water for several minutes in between rinses. Taste. You want it just slightly sweet and salty. Drain in a sieve.

Place a medium frying pan over medium heat. Once hot, add the *chai poh* and push it around for 2-3 minutes, until fragrant and faintly scorched. Introduce the lard or oil, followed by the garlic. Lower the heat slightly and fry until the garlic turns pale gold.

Add the light soy sauce. Once absorbed by the pan's contents, turn off the heat. Decant into a bowl and serve with the *chwee kueh*.

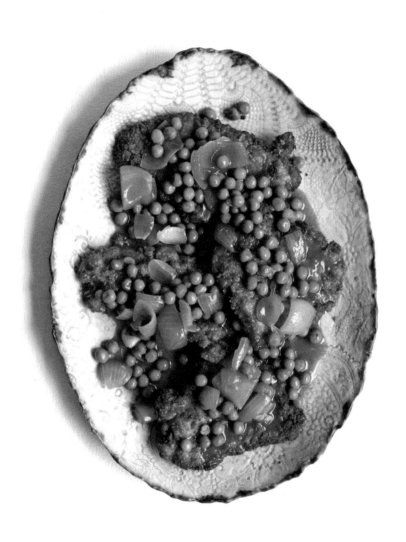

HAINANESE PORK CUTLETS

When the Hainanese arrived in Singapore during the second half of the 19th century in search of work, the majority got jobs in army cookhouses, hotels and British households, where they were exposed to Western ingredients, such as mustard and Worcestershire sauce, cooking techniques and dishes. This is their interpretation of one such dish, which became something of a stalwart at Hainanese-owned coffee shops, the earliest of which is said to have opened in the 1930s. Just the sight of these cutlets conjures up images of marble-topped wooden tables and glossy tiled walls.

SERVES 4

4 x 100g pork loin pieces
Peanut oil, for frying

for the marinade
2 tsp Worchestershire sauce
1 tbsp oyster sauce
1 garlic clove, peeled and minced
1 tbsp Shaoxing rice wine
¼ tsp finely ground black pepper

for the sauce
1 tbsp unsalted butter
2 yellow onions, peeled and cut into
    rough chunks
225g frozen peas
3 tbsp HP sauce
3 tbsp tomato ketchup
2 tsp light soy sauce
1 tbsp oyster sauce
1 tbsp Worchestershire sauce
400ml good beef stock
2 tsp light brown sugar
2 tbsp cornflour, made into a slurry
    with 2 tbsp water
Salt, finely ground black pepper

for coating
75g plain flour
2 eggs, lightly beaten
200g cream crackers, finely crushed

Begin the day before you wish to eat. Flatten the pork loin pieces by placing them on a chopping board and thwacking them with a rolling pin, mallet or tenderiser into cutlets approximately ½cm thick. Place these in a tray, add the marinade ingredients and massage. Cover and refrigerate overnight.

The following day, remove the pork from the cold. While it loses its chill, make the sauce. Heat the butter in a medium saucepan over medium heat. Add the onions and fry until they have just begun to soften. Add the frozen peas, HP sauce, tomato ketchup, light soy, oyster and Worchestershire sauces, beef stock and light brown sugar. Once the mixture boils, reduce the heat and simmer for 5 minutes. Stir in the cornflour slurry. The sauce will thicken in seconds, but let it simmer for 2-3 minutes before removing from the heat. Adjust seasoning with salt and black pepper.

Place 3 shallow bowls on your counter. Contain the plain flour in one and season with a little salt and black pepper. Crack the eggs into another and lightly beat. Place the crushed cream crackers in the final bowl.

Turn the cutlets over in the flour, then the beaten egg and lastly the crushed cream crackers, ensuring they are well coated. Arrange them on a tray.

Heat 4cm of peanut oil in a large frying pan over medium heat. Once hot, but not smoking, fry the cutlets for 3-4 minutes, to a rich golden turn, turning them over midway. Drain them on kitchen towel to remove excess oil, then arrange on a serving platter.

Reheat the sauce and nap the cutlets with it. Any remaining sauce may be tipped into a bowl, jug or somesuch vessel and served alongside.

TARO RICE 芋头饭

Versions of this sold in food courts so often taste mostly of soy and dried shrimp, when it should be bosky with shiitake, meaty with lap cheong and dulcet with powdery cubes of taro.

It happens to be quite the one-pot wonder, requiring no supporting cast, save a small bowl of sambal belacan (page 219). One caveat, however: you require a rice cooker. I have not yet been able to replicate its success on the stove.

SERVES 6

6 dried shiitake mushrooms
3 tbsp vegetable oil
4 shallots, peeled and finely sliced
3 garlic cloves, peeled and chopped
25g dried shrimp, soaked and
    roughly chopped (page 219)
2 Chinese sausages (*lap cheong*), cut
    into ½cm slices on a gentle bias
350g jasmine rice, washed and drained
2 tbsp Shaoxing rice wine
1½ tbsp light soy sauce
1½ tbsp dark soy sauce
1 tbsp oyster sauce
¼ tsp caster sugar
Finely ground white pepper
250g taro yam, peeled and cut into
    1½cm cubes
2 spring onions, finely sliced

Soak the shiitake mushrooms in 250ml boiling water for 15 minutes, then drain, reserving the soaking liquor. Remove the stalks from the mushrooms and dice their caps.

Heat the vegetable oil in a wide saucepan or wok over medium heat. Once hot, add the shallots and fry until crisp and golden, lowering the heat slightly midway. Convey the shallots to a plate lined with kitchen towel.

To the shallot-infused oil in the saucepan, add the garlic. Fry over medium heat, until fragrant but lightly coloured, then add the dried shrimp. Fry for 2 minutes, then add the prepared shiitake mushrooms and *lap cheong* and fry for another minute.

Now add the rice, pushing the grains around for 30 seconds, then add the Shaoxing rice wine, light and dark soy sauces, oyster sauce, caster sugar and a dash of ground white pepper. Finally mix in the cubed taro and tip everything into a rice cooker.

Strain the shiitake soaking liquor into a measuring jug and add water to reach the 475ml mark. Pour this liquid over the rice and cook as you would regular white grains. Leave for 30 minutes for the taro rice to compose itself.

Gently stir to redistribute the ingredients and plate up. Sprinkle with spring onions and the recently fried shallots.

MEE TAI BAK SOUP

The broth for this is quite light and clean-tasting. For something a bit more full-bodied, you may replace the carcasses entirely with chicken wings or indeed use a whole chicken instead, allowing its shredded flesh to replace the pork mince. You could also add some blanched pork ribs or bones for a different brand of savouriness.

In place of the tai bak, what in Chinese is known as lao shu fen, "rat's tail noodles", you may use rice vermicelli (bee hoon) or flat rice noodles (kway teow).

SERVES 4

for the broth
750g chicken carcasses
500g chicken wings
2½ litres water
2 garlic cloves, unpeeled
2cm ginger, lightly crushed
4 spring onions
1 tsp salt, plus more to taste
½ tsp white peppercorns

for the pork
75g pork mince
1 tsp light soy sauce
2 tsp Shaoxing rice wine
A few drops of toasted sesame oil
Pinch of salt
Pinch of finely ground white pepper

to finish
400g mee tai bak
8 good quality fishballs, cooked
2 tbsp crisp-fried shallots (page 220)
Small bunch of coriander, coarsely
    chopped
4 spring onions, finely sliced

Combine the ingredients for the broth in a large pot. Place over high heat, bring to a boil, then cover, reduce the heat and simmer very gently for 3 hours, returning occasionally to skim off any scum.

Strain the broth into a fresh pot. Skim off as much fat as possible, then taste and season with salt.

Combine the ingredients for the pork in a bowl and gently mix. Cover and refrigerate for 30 minutes.

Place the *mee tai bak* and fish balls in a small colander and throw over a cup or so of boiling water, just to awaken them. (You could alternatively quickly blanch both in a small saucepan of boiling water.)

Bring the stock to a rolling boil. Add the seasoned pork mince in lumps, stirring to break them up. Once the meat is opaque, which should take no longer than several seconds, add the *mee tai bak* and fishballs. Simmer for just half a minute or so, to warm them up.

Divide among 4 bowls. Sprinkle with crisp-fried shallots, coriander and spring onions. Serve with little saucers of sliced red bird's eye chillies and light soy sauce.

TEOCHEW FISH PORRIDGE 潮州鱼粥

Teochew cuisine has a reputation for being clean-tasting, which some unfairly view as a euphemism for bland. Delicacy is not the absence of personality and it takes skill to keep the flavour profile lean yet nuanced and sharp.

Some merely resuscitate cooked rice in hot stock before adding the fish, while others simmer the rice for longer, breaking the grains down a little while imbuing them with more flavour. I am with the latter camp. I use a clean-flavoured chicken stock and dried anchovies, shrimp, cuttlefish and dover sole, all aligned with Teochew cooking sensibilities. Some cooks finely sliver and fry the dried cuttlefish before adding it to the pot. You may do so if you wish, as it does provide an injection of sweet savouriness. I, however, am not in the habit.

SERVES 6

for the stock
500g chicken wings
1 garlic clove, peeled
2cm ginger, peeled and crushed
1 tsp salt, plus more to taste
1¼ litres water
25g dried anchovies
10g dried shrimp
1 quill of dried sole, toasted (page 218)
1 piece of dried cuttlefish
2 spring onions

for the fish
250g Spanish mackerel, deboned
    and sliced
2cm ginger, peeled and finely slivered
¼ tsp salt
½ tsp light soy sauce
½ tsp cornflour
Finely ground white pepper

Begin with the stock. Combine the chicken wings, garlic, ginger, salt and water in a large pot. Place over medium-high heat, bring to a boil, then lower the heat, cover and simmer gently for 1½ hours.

Rinse the dried anchovies and shrimp separately, to rid them of surfeit salt. Lightly toast both in a small frying pan until fragrant, but not coloured.

Add the prepared dried anchovies and shrimp to the stock, along with the toasted dried sole, dried cuttlefish and spring onions. Cover and simmer for another 25 minutes.

Meanwhile, combine the sliced Spanish mackerel with the ginger, salt, light soy sauce, cornflour and a dash of ground white pepper. Cover and refrigerate until needed.

When the broth is done, strain it through a fine mesh sieve into a large heatproof jug. Skim off as much fat as possible. Return 850ml to the pot, reserving any extra for thinning later.

to cook
300g cooked jasmine rice
½ tsp light soy sauce
½ tsp fish sauce

to serve
Crisp-fried garlic (page 219)
Spring onions, finely sliced
***You tiao* (page 33)**

Add the rice to the pot and simmer over medium-low heat for 15 minutes without a lid. Add the light soy and fish sauces, and simmer for another 10 minutes, again sans lid, until the rice has absorbed most of the liquid but is still juicy.

Add the fish to the pot. Cook for 3-4 minutes until the fish is opaque. There should be a shimmering layer of liquid on the surface of the porridge. Add a little of the reserved stock if need be. (The porridge will thicken as it sits, so loosen it with more of the reserved stock as you see fit. If you have used up all the stock, some boiling water will do.) Taste and tweak seasoning with salt.

Serve promptly with crisp-fried garlic, sliced spring onions and, of course, *you tiao*.

YOU TIAO 油条

I always thought these were difficult to make but as it turns out I had confused skill with patience.

Besides accompanying many a rice porridge, these complete tau suan (page 125). They are also quite good plunged into mugs of sweet, hot coffee, a typical breakfast or snack for many in Southeast Asia. Some grease inevitably winds up in the drink but perhaps it is insouciance that makes this manner of consumption even more appealing.

MAKES 8

300g plain flour
1½ tsp baking powder
¼ tsp baking soda
¼ tsp salt
Pinch of caster sugar
1 egg, lightly beaten
1 tbsp unsalted butter, softened
60ml milk
50ml water
Peanut oil, for deep-frying

In a freestanding electric mixer fitted with a dough hook, place the plain flour, baking powder and soda, salt and caster sugar. Let the machine whir for several seconds, just to combine the dry ingredients, then add the egg, unsalted butter, milk and water. Operate at a medium speed, until a moist, cohesive dough is obtained. Cover the bowl and leave for 15 minutes.

Uncover the bowl and, at a medium speed, knead the dough for 8-10 minutes, until smooth, elastic, very soft but not sticky. You may add a tad more water if necessary. Transfer the dough out onto a work surface and fashion it into an oblong. Wrap it well in clingfilm and refrigerate for at least 8 hours or overnight.

The following day, remove the dough from the fridge and leave it on the counter for an hour or so to return to room temperature.

Uncloak the dough and place it on a lightly floured work surface. Give it a brief massage, then stretch it out into a 12 x 32 x ½cm rectangle. Lightly dust the dough's surface with flour, trim off any irregularities from its edges, then cut it horizontally into 16 x 2cm-wide strips. Pair up these strips, resting one on top of the other. Brand them, right down their middles, with a slim chopstick or metal skewer so their edges fan out.

Pour enough peanut oil in a 25cm-wide, deep frying pan or wok to reach a 5cm depth and place over medium heat. Once the fat is hot, attaining a temperature of 200°C, take one *you tiao*, hold it above the pan, gently stretch it to a 22cm-length, then lower it into the hot fat. Fry for 2-3 minutes until puffy and golden, constantly turning it with chopsticks. Drain on a plate lined with kitchen towel. Fry the remaining *you tiao* in this manner, 2-3 at a time.

ACAR AWAK

This version of Nyonya vegetable pickles is notably robust with sesame and peanuts, which blunts the spikes of the vinegar and spices, in particular the turmeric, whose voice seems to ring with especial clarity.

The batons into which the cucumber and carrot are cut should be on the thick side as they shrink considerably after most of their moisture has been removed.

MAKES approx. 1kg

for the vegetables
225g cucumber, cut into 4cm batons
225g carrot, cut into 4cm batons
150g cabbage, cut into large chunks
175g cauliflower, broken into florets
100g yardlong beans, cut into 4cm
    sections
125g shallots, peeled
250ml white cane vinegar
500ml water
1 tsp salt
8 green chillies

for the spice paste
20g garlic cloves, peeled
100g shallots, peeled and sliced
15g fresh turmeric, peeled
25g galangal, peeled and sliced
2 lemongrass stalks, tender portion
    only, sliced
150g red chillies, sliced
8 dried chillies, softened (page 218)
2 candlenuts
1½ tsp fermented shrimp paste
    (*belacan*), toasted (page 219)

to cook
150ml vegetable oil
1 tsp salt
125g caster sugar
250ml white cane vinegar

to finish
175g peanuts, skinned, roasted
    and chopped (page 220)
75g sesame seeds, toasted (page 220)

Begin with the vegetables. Place the cucumber and carrot in 2 separate bowls. Sprinkle each with ½ tsp salt and leave for 30 minutes. After this period, they would have exuded a lot of liquid, so drain and squeeze them separately to expel as much moisture as possible. Spread them out on a tray lined with tea towel and sun for 3-4 hours, to dry out slightly.

Prepare the cabbage, cauliflower, yardlong beans and shallots as described. Prepare an ice bath. Bring the 250ml white cane vinegar, 500ml water and 1 tsp salt to a boil in a medium-sized saucepan. Blanch each of the 4 prepared vegetables, as well as the green chillies, in batches for just 10 seconds, then plunge them into the ice bath. Squeeze them dry and arrange on a fresh tray lined with tea towel.

Pound the ingredients for the spice paste with a pestle and mortar until fine, or blitz them in a cosy blender, adding a tiny bit of water if necessary.

Heat the oil in a large wok or saucepan over medium heat. Once hot but not smoking, add the spice paste. Fry for a minute, then lower the heat and fry for 10 minutes, or until deep red, fragrant and separated from the oil. Add the 1 tsp salt and the caster sugar, followed by the 250ml white cane vinegar. Bring to a boil, then reduce the heat and simmer for 2-3 minutes to cook out the rawness from the vinegar. Turn off the heat and stir in all the vegetables – the sunned cucumber and carrot, the blanched cabbage, cauliflower, yardlong beans, shallots and green chillies. Leave the vegetables to cool in the pan, then stir in the peanuts and sesame. Taste and adjust seasoning with salt.

This is best consumed at least 24 hours after making. Kept in a sterilised jar in the refrigerator, it will last for up to 1-2 months.

AYAM GORENG

This recipe was inspired by the fried chicken that my mother's company driver, Sanusi bin Damiri, would often have for lunch, bolstered with a mesa of hot rice. I would watch him relish the contents of the brown paper parcel at the kitchen table while trudging through primary school homework. He began getting an extra parcel upon noticing my curiosity at what I then regarded to be a rather luxurious repast. It was from our time together that I learned how to eat with my hands.

SERVES 6-8

500g chicken drumsticks and wings
Peanut oil, for deep-frying

for the spice paste
1 tbsp coriander seeds
1 tbsp cumin seeds
2 tsp fennel seeds
6 cardamom pods
½ tsp white peppercorns
1 tsp ground turmeric
5 garlic cloves, peeled
30g shallots, peeled
30g ginger, peeled and sliced
35g galangal, peeled and sliced
1cm fresh turmeric, peeled
1 lemongrass stalk, tender portion only, sliced
1 egg, beaten
1 tsp light soy sauce
½ tsp salt
½ tsp caster sugar

for the coating
200g cornflour
25g potato starch
15g plain flour
Pinch of baking soda
4 tbsp water

Arrange the chicken pieces in a wide dish and pierce them all over with a fine metal skewer.

Lightly toast the coriander, cumin and fennel seeds, cardamom pods and white peppercorns in a small frying pan over medium-low heat until aromatic. Crush with a pestle and mortar into a powder and sprinkle, along with the ground turmeric, over the chicken.

Use the pestle and mortar to pound the garlic, shallots, ginger, galangal, fresh turmeric and lemongrass into a fine paste. Add this, the egg, light soy sauce, salt and caster sugar to the chicken. Massage thoroughly. Cover and leave to marinate overnight.

The following day, remove the chicken 30 minutes before cooking. Combine the cornflour, potato starch, plain flour and baking soda in a small bowl then sprinkle over the chicken, followed by the water. Mix until the pieces are well coated. The batter will be slippery and defiant, coating the chicken with unnerving unevenness. It will also appear slightly reddish, due to the reaction between the soda and turmeric.

Heat 5cm cooking oil in a wide, deep frying pan (or wok) over medium heat. Once the oil is hot, or when the tip of an inserted chopstick is devoured by fine bubbles, fry the chicken pieces in batches until golden and cooked-through, 12-15 minutes. Convey these to a tray lined with kitchen towel. Cool for a couple of minutes before eating.

KUIH KODOK

Kodok, in Malay, means "toad", which is what these freeform doughnuts of banana are thought to resemble. They are also known as cekodok pisang or jemput–jemput.

The traditional banana for this is pisang awak, but here I use pisang mas, lady finger bananas. Truthfully, any ripe (or, even better, overripe) banana will work here.

I used to eat these cold in the car on the way home from school but they are undeniably at their peak fresh from the pan. If you think time is cruel to humans, then just watch how it smites these.

MAKES 18-20

200g ripe lady finger bananas, peeled weight
35g caster sugar
50g plain flour
25g rice flour
Pinch of baking soda
Pinch of salt
Peanut oil, for deep-frying

In a medium-sized mixing bowl, crush the banana flesh into a pulp with the caster sugar. Stir in the plain and rice flours, baking soda and salt until a thick batter is obtained.

Fill a medium-sized saucepan with 3cm peanut oil and place over medium heat. Once the fat is adequately hot – an inserted chopstick should be consumed by fine bubbles – drop several bulging teaspoonfuls of banana batter in separate areas of the pan. You want them to swell, rise and steadily turn deep gold, about 3-4 minutes. Convey them to a tray lined generously with kitchen towel. (They can be quite greasy.) Continue making the rest of the *kodok* this way.

BUBUR TERIGU

Terigu refers to white wheat berries, the word derived from the Portuguese trigo. They are also called biji gandum. In terms of texture, they pack a fleshier chew than barley, and are also earthier, creating a futon of mustiness so dense that large quantities of gula melaka and pandan leaves are needed to combat it.

This version of bubur terigu includes sago pearls. Counterintuitively, they brighten the porridge, the constellation of tiny, transparent eyes punctuating every mouthful with bursts of dewy freshness .

SERVES 4-6

125g white wheat berries (*terigu*)
1¼ litres water
3 pandan blades, knotted
90g sago pearls
200g coconut sugar (*gula melaka*), shaved
¼ tsp salt
125ml coconut cream, plus more to serve

Wash the white wheat several times until the water runs clear. Place them in a bowl and cover generously with water. Soak for 4-5 hours, or until the grains are easily crushed between fingers.

Drain the white wheat and put them in a medium-sized saucepan. Add the 1¼ litres water, bring to a boil over high heat, then stick in the pandan blades. Cover, lower the heat and simmer gently until the wheat is tender, the liquid slightly thickened.

Stir in the sago pearls, cover again, and simmer until these are mostly cooked: the tiny white eyes they will possess, like small cataracts, are desirable at this stage and tend to disappear by serving time.

Add the shaved *gula melaka* and salt. Once the sugar melts, add the coconut cream and cook the *bubur* for just 1-2 more minutes.

Divide among 4-6 bowls and serve with a jug of coconut cream for those who want more.

KUIH LOPES

In judicious quantities, the alkaline water, which may be easily procured from Asian grocers, gives the cooked and cooled dumpling a delectable, gelatinous crunch. Go overboard, however, and you will be met with biting soapiness.

This substance is also responsible for the cakes' jaundiced hue, producing an uncommitted chartreuse that cooks usually anchor with drops of yellow food colouring. I do not bother with this, but the call is yours. Crushed dried gardenia fruits, available at Chinese medicine shops, make a fine, natural alternative to E numbers but I have not had the chance to put them to the test yet.

MAKES 6

300g glutinous rice
600ml water
2 tsp alkaline water
A few drops of yellow food colouring, optional
2 tsp caster sugar
2 tsp vegetable oil
Pinch of salt
Six 12x24cm banana leaf rectangles, softened (page 218)

for the syrup
150g coconut sugar (*gula melaka*), shaved
1 pandan blade, knotted
200ml water

for the coconut
150g grated coconut
A pinch of salt

Wash the glutinous rice three times or until the water runs clear. Place them in a bowl, then cover with 300ml of the water. Sprinkle in the alkaline water and the yellow food colouring if using. Cover and leave for 8-10 hours or overnight.

The following day, drain the rice and place it in a wide saucepan or deep frying pan. Stir in the remaining 300ml water, caster sugar, vegetable oil and salt. Place the pan over medium heat and cook, stirring, until you get a thick beaded mixture, like a congealed (and somewhat crunchy) risotto. Divide this into 6 portions.

Take one rectangle of banana leaf and shape it into a cornet. Press in a portion of the half-cooked rice, then fold over the outstanding portions of leaf to form a compact triangular parcel. Secure the parcel with string. Make all the *lopes* this way.

Prepare your steamer, filling its lower compartment with plenty of water and placing it over high heat.

Steam the *lopes* for 45 minutes, replenishing the water in the lower compartment if necessary.

Meanwhile, make the syrup by combining the shaved coconut sugar, pandan blade and water in a saucepan over medium heat. Once the sugar has dissolved, continue simmering the syrup for 5 minutes, or until it has reduced slightly and the pandan blade looks scalded and spent. Strain this dark syrup into a jug.

Contain the grated coconut in a heatproof dish befitting of your steamer and fork in the salt.

Remove the parcels of *lopes* from the steamer and allow them to cool slightly. Lower the dish of salted grated coconut into the freshly vacated steamer and steam for just 3-4 minutes to heat it through.

To serve, unwrap the rice cakes, roll them in the grated coconut and arrange them on a serving platter. Take them to the table with the jug of *gula melaka* syrup.

SWEETCORN ICE CREAM

My fondness for sweet ices goes back decades. On afternoons, outside the school gate, an ice cream vendor would wait beneath the pantone umbrella of his mobile kiosk, essentially a portable freezer trunk attached to the back of a bicycle, the sharp tinkling of his bell a sign of his arrival.

The pictorial menus of such ambulant vendors would indicate about a dozen offerings, most of them set in cardboard-bound blocks. My favourites have not changed since young: red bean, raspberry ripple, durian, mint chip and sweetcorn. These ice creams are usually softly flavoured, more milky than creamy. I suspect that for the majority contending with tropical climes and humidity, it is this general lightness that ticks many boxes.

When a selection is made, a block of ice cream would be retrieved from the freezer, still protected by its carton, and placed on a small wooden board. A nifty cleaver would remove a slab from its body, a deft pair of fingers would strip off the bit of cardboard lining it. The frosty, slowly melting, slab will then be promptly shunt between a pair of thin, disproportionately sized, wafers or into the fold of a pappy, rainbow-hued sandwich bread slice.

Making sweetcorn ice cream from scratch is not difficult but takes effort. The complexities of sweetcorn are easily drowned out when seized in frozen custard, which is why many resort to bottled essences. This is my attempt to recreate the taste of this childhood treat without enlisting any of these potions.

Although I do not set it in a block, I have retained the gentle iciness of old-fashioned ice creams. It is a quality that affords a soupçon of rusticity, of innocence, which, in this context, I find entirely desirable.

SERVES 4-6

4 sweetcorn cobs
300ml millk
100ml whipping cream
1 pandan blade, snipped
3 egg yolks
80g caster sugar
Pinch of salt
60ml coconut cream
2 tsp good quality unsalted butter

Remove the husks from the sweetcorn cobs and shave their kernels into a bowl. Do not discard the denuded cobs just yet.

Weigh the kernels: you want 700g. Remove 50g and finely chop these. Set aside.

Tip the remaining 650g into a liquidiser and blend into a smoothie-like consistency. Squeeze this liquid in a muslin in batches to extract as much corn milk as possible. This does take time but is relatively easy work. The fibre remaining in the muslin should be discarded. Strain the corn milk through a sieve into a measuring jug. You need 350ml of corn milk; I suppose any excess may be drunk.

Combine the (regular) milk and whipping cream in a medium-sized saucepan and break in as many of the denuded cobs as the pan allows. Add the snipped pandan blade. Place the pan over low heat and simmer gently for 10 minutes, then tong out the sweetcorn cobs and pandan.

Give the corn milk a whisk – the starch tends to settle at the bottom of the jug – and pour it into the infused milk and cream in the saucepan. Cook over medium-low heat until it thickens into a brilliant yellow cream, like an exaggeratedly hued lemon curd. Take off the heat for now.

In a small bowl, beat the egg yolks, caster sugar and salt until pale yellow and thick. Scrape this into the thick corn cream and whisk immediately. Return the pan to a low heat and simmer gently, whisking, until it thickens even further.

Add the chopped corn kernels, cook for 2 minutes, then finally the coconut cream and unsalted butter. Once the butter has melted, remove the pan from the heat. Have a taste; it should be a notch sweeter than preferred.

Scrape the corn custard into a bowl, allow it to cool completely, then churn in an ice cream maker according to the manufacturer's instructions. Convey the ice cream to a suitably sized Tupperware or somesuch container and stash it in the freezer. This ice cream keeps well for up to a week.

THE BOTTLE BLUE

My maternal grandmother, who was born in Ipoh and spent many years in Penang, had a reputation for being a formidable cook. Unfortunately, by the time I made the kitchen my safe haven, she was in her seventies and had surrendered the apron. What I know of her prowess has been gleaned from conversations with my mother, who would assist her in the kitchen when she was much younger, from the cleaning of gizzards to the rendering of lard, the toasting of fermented shrimp paste (*belacan*) to the meticulous shredding of dried cuttlefish (*juhu*). The recipes in this chapter are heavily based on these conversations.

Despite never getting to witness her acumen first hand, my grandmother's persnicketiness towards food was hard to miss. She would often supervise the domestic helpers when they prepared dinner, ensuring the *rempah* for the curry was adequately fried, that the coconut milk did not come from packets, that the batons of cucumber and carrots were uniform.

She also had the ability to turn simple tasks into artforms. A fine example was the making of toast. After freeing two squares of plastic bread from their frames, she would offer them to a toaster oven set to purring heat until they were hard, hollow and almost black. She would let these cinder coasters cool on a wire rack before holding them over the sink and scraping off their charred skins. She would then paint them, with immense care and devotion, with a layer of peanut butter, and another of strawberry jam. She would then arrange these decorated tiles, side by side, on her favourite plate, supported by a mug of milky brew, prepared with two black tea bags, absolutely no water and easily a quarter-cup of sugar.

KERABU MANGGA

This is how my grandmother made her green mango salad.
I prefer using a knife to turn the fruit into shreds; the irregularity makes the kerabu eat more satisfyingly. You may use a papaya shredder, like a vegetable peeler with ridged blades, easily purchased from Thai grocers.

SERVES 4

2 tsp dried shrimp, softened
   (page 219)
2 red bird's eye chillies, finely sliced
1 heaped tsp fermented shrimp paste
   (*belacan*), toasted (page 219)
1 tbsp caster sugar, plus more to taste
1 tbsp calamansi lime juice
A medium green mango, approx.
   200g
3 shallots, peeled and thinly sliced
1 torch ginger bud, thinly sliced
   or finely chopped
Salt

Soak the dried shrimp in a bowl of cold water for 5 minutes. Drain thoroughly and pound into a floss with a pestle and mortar. Toast this floss in a small frying pan over medium heat until aromatic, then tip into a bowl and set aside.

Add the red bird's eye chillies and fermented shrimp paste to the vacated mortar. Pound into a paste, then work in the caster sugar and calamansi lime juice. Set aside.

Peel the green mango. With a sharp knife, hack away at it, covering it in myriad wounds running (more or less) parallel to one another. Run the knife against its flesh, sending rough slivers into a capacious bowl.

Add the shrimp floss, chilli paste, shallots and torch ginger bud. Toss until the mango is well-coated; you may add 1-2 tbsp water if you find it too tightly dressed. Taste and adjust seasoning with salt and sugar.

KERABU NANAS

Pineapple with pale yellow flesh, on the cusp of ripeness, is ideal. It has the brightness and sharpness to stand up to the chilli and sugar, which should be granulated; the soft, fading crunch of the cystals adds another dimension to the experience. If your fruit is properly ripe, all is not lost, just reduce the sugar slightly or omit it entirely. We often buy pineapple ready-peeled and without eyes. This recipe takes this into account.

My mother loves this with hot rice and fried fish.

SERVES 4

400g pineapple flesh, peeled weight
   (see above)
2 tbsp dark soy sauce
1 tsp fermented shrimp paste
   (*belacan*), toasted (page 219)
2 red bird's eye chillies, finely sliced
1 tbsp granulated sugar
1 tbsp mint leaves
2-3 calamansi limes, halved

Cut the pineapple flesh into boat shapes. Incise out their tough portions (the core), then cut their flesh at 1cm intervals into triangularish chips. Place in a bowl.

Work the dark soy sauce and toasted fermented shrimp paste into a smooth, treacle-dark ointment with a pestle and mortar. Add this, together with the red bird's eye chillies, to the pineapple and mix well.

Convey to a serving dish and sprinkle with the granulated sugar and mint leaves. Serve with the calamansi limes for folks who desire more acidity.

KERABU SOTONG

A simple but effective salad, one you are likely to find in the northeastern Malaysian state of Kelantan, brushing against the Thai border, bolstered with cooked beanthread noodles.

The sweetness of the squid is accentuated by the acidity of the calamansi lime juice which, mixed with a little sugar and salt, makes for a breezy but pointed little dressing. Resist the urge to taint it with fish sauce. You may, however, herb it up with coriander or mint.

SERVES 2

2 medium squid, total weight
    approx. 250g
3 shallots, peeled and thinly sliced
2 lemongrass stalks, tender portion
    only, thinly sliced
2 red bird's eye chillies, finely sliced
1 small cucumber, deseeded and cut
    into thin slices
3 tbsp calamansi lime juice
¼ tsp caster sugar
Pinch or so of salt
A dash of freshly ground black pepper

Pull the wings off the squid and remove their purplish skins. Tug out their arms and cut off anything above their eyes, also removing their beaks. Cut their arms into shorter sections.

Skin their tubular bodies, cut them open and scrape out the innards. Score in a criss-cross fashion, then cut into shorter sections.

Bring a medium saucepan of water to a boil, then drop in the squid. The moment they curl up, remove them to a bowl. Allow them to cool for a minute or so, then mix in the shallots, lemongrass, bird's eye chillies, cucumber, calamansi lime juice, caster sugar, salt and black pepper. Taste and adjust seasoning.

UDANG MASAK LEMAK NANAS

I was only acquainted with the more lavishly gravied version of this, prawns cooked with spices, pineapple and coconut milk, a little later in life. The one made under my grandmother's supervision was always quite dry, with a small dollop of coconut cream swirled in towards the end. Fresh coconut cream is ideal, but given the required quantity, I would not lose too much sleep if it did ooze out from a carton.

Everyone is keen on large prawns these days but I think medium-sized ones are more suitable here. Apart from being sweeter, their tightly curled bodies, nestled in the bowl of a spoon, red sauce hugging them, eat more elegantly. In our home, we peel them entirely, but you may leave their tails on, as is commonly done.

Ripe pineapple works best here. The finishing frisson of slivered makrut lime leaves is not common, but my grandmother always added it.

SERVES 4

for the spice paste
2 garlic cloves, peeled
4 shallots, peeled
75g red chillies, sliced
3 bird's eye chillies
1 lemongrass stalk, tender
   portion only
1 tsp fermented shrimp paste
   (*belacan*), toasted (page 219)

for cooking
5 tbsp vegetable oil
350g medium prawns, peeled weight
¼ tsp salt, plus more to taste
175g ripe pineapple flesh, peeled
   weight, cut into chunks
2 tbsp tamarind water (page 221)
3 tbsp coconut cream (see above)
4 makrut lime leaves, finely slivered
Caster sugar, to taste

Make the spice paste by pounding the ingredients together with a pestle and mortar until fine and smooth. Alternatively, blitz them in a cosy blender, adding a tiny bit of water to help them along if necessary.

Heat the oil in a wok or large frying pan over medium-high heat. Once hot, add the spice paste. Fry for a minute, stirring constantly. Reduce the heat to medium-low and continue frying until the paste splits in the oil, arrives at an intense red and is warmly fragrant.

Stir in the peeled prawns. Cook for several seconds, just until the prawns turn slightly opaque, then add the salt, pineapple and tamarind water. Cook for just 2-3 minutes, until the prawns have curled up and the pineapple has been warmed through and is slightly softened. Stir in the coconut cream and makrut lime leaves. Cook for a final 30 seconds, then remove the pan from the heat. Taste and adjust seasoning with salt and sugar.

IKAN KUNING GORENG KUNYIT

This is a simple but utterly delicious way to treat yellowstripe scad (ikan kuning selar), with their striking silver bodies. The fish I use are those 10–12cm in length, typically served with nasi lemak. Anything larger and you will have to score them a couple of times on each side.

My grandmother would typically use tamarind water that is quite thick, almost paste-like, which half-heartedly clings onto the fish as it fries, turning black and slightly sticky. To make this, dissolve 25g tamarind pulp in 75ml hot water and push it through a sieve, adding just a little more water to help it along.

Instead of tamarind, a squirt of calamansi lime juice will do just fine.

SERVES 4

250g small yellowstripe scad
(*ikan kuning selar*), cleaned
½ tsp salt
1 tsp ground turmeric
3 tbsp thick tamarind water
(see above)
Peanut oil, for deep-frying

With gloved hands, rub the cleaned fish with the salt, ground turmeric and thick tamarind water. Cover and refrigerate for 1 hour.

Heat 2cm of peanut oil in a wide, deep frying pan or wok over medium-high heat. Once hot, deep-fry the fish in batches, until dark brown and crisp, about 6-8 minutes, turning over midway. Drain on kitchen towel and eat while hot.

OTAK-OTAK

I grew up eating two main kinds of otak-otak ("brains" in Malay) in Singapore, both involving a spiced paste of fish. The first kind presents itself as oblong banana leaf parcels, the second svelte rulers of nipa palm blade. And while the first may either be steamed or grilled, the second is always grilled.

The version my mother grew up eating was different, however. The custard in the Penang otak contains chunks of fish and receives additional perfume from daun kaduk, wild betel leaves. When fresh, the deep green, heart-shaped blades of Piper sarmentosum are sweetly medicinal, with notes of clove, mint and liquorice. When heated, this scent transforms, turning herbaceous, evoking wet fields and rivers, in the best possible way. In addition to wild betel, I add makrut lime leaves. Some cooks add turmeric leaves, too.

Indian threadfin (kurau) and Spanish mackerel (tenggiri batang) are popular fishes to use, but any with clean-tasting and firm white flesh will do. Not all recipes use belacan, but the pinprick of putridity imparted by a small, toasted nugget is quite appetising.

MAKES 6

for the spice paste
2 garlic cloves, peeled
50g shallots, peeled weight
50g red chillies, sliced
3 dried chillies, deseeded and softened
   (page 218)
2 candlenuts
2 lemongrass stalks, tender portion
   only, thinly sliced
10g galangal, peeled weight, sliced
5g turmeric, peeled weight, sliced
½ tsp fermented shrimp paste
   (belacan), toasted (page 219)

for the filling
100ml coconut cream
2 tsp light brown sugar
1 egg, beaten
1 tbsp rice flour
¼ tsp salt
A few drops of fish sauce
6 makrut lime leaves, deveined and
   thinly slivered
250g threadfin fillet, skinned and
   deboned weight, cut into 2cm pieces
Six 18x22cm banana leaf rectangles,
   softened (page 218)
12 wild betel leaves

Make the spice paste by pounding the ingredients together with a pestle and mortar until fine and smooth. Alternatively, blitz them in a cosy blender, adding a tiny bit of water to help them along if necessary.

Tip the spice paste into a bowl. Mix in the coconut cream, light brown sugar, egg, rice flour, salt, fish sauce and makrut lime leaves. Stir in the threadfin pieces.

Place a softened sheet of banana leaf on the work surface before you. Rest 2 wild betel leaves on it, side by side, and dollop on a sixth – about 3 tbsp – of the spicy fish mixture. Lift the top and bottom edges of the leaf to meet one another, then tuck in the right and left sides to form a tent-like pouch and secure with a toothpick or two. Make all the parcels this way.

Prepare your steamer, filling it with plenty of water and putting it over medium-high heat. Once boiling, arrange the parcels in the perforated compartment and steam for 10-12 minutes.

Cool slightly before defrocking.

KARI AYAM

Some people like the gravy for their chicken curry thick enough to coat their palates. I prefer mine to barely hug a spoon.

Great though the combination of rice and curry is, I prefer eating this – the chicken flesh ripped into shreds, the potatoes crushed into a balm – with roti perancis ("French loaves") or crusty baguettes. A plate of roti jala would not go astray, either.

SERVES 6-8

for the spice paste
20g garlic cloves, peeled
125g shallots, peeled and sliced
2 red chillies, sliced
10 dried chillies, deseeded and
    softened (page 218)
20g ginger, peeeled and sliced
25g galangal, peeled and sliced
25g turmeric, peeled and sliced
2 candlenuts
1 tsp fermented shrimp paste
    (*belacan*), toasted (page 219)

for the dry spices
½ tsp cumin seeds
3 tbsp coriander seeds
1 tbsp fennel seeds
6 green cardamom pods
4 cloves
1 star anise
3cm cinnamon stick
¼ tsp white peppercorns
¼ tsp black peppercorns
1 tsp ground turmeric
2 tsp Kashmiri chilli powder
4 tbsp water

to cook
300g waxy potatoes, peeled and
    quartered
100ml vegetable oil
2 lemongrass stalks, bruised
1.4kg chicken, jointed into 10
1½ tsp salt, plus more to taste
1½ tsp caster sugar
1 tbsp light soy sauce
500ml coconut milk
150ml coconut cream
20 curry leaves

Make the spice paste by pounding everything with a pestle and mortar or blitzing in a cosy blender with a tiny bit of water to help the ingredients along. Set aside.

In a frying pan, toast the cumin, coriander and fennel seeds, cardamom pods, cloves, star anise, cinnamon and peppercorns. Once aromatic and faintly toasted, cool slightly, then crush into a fine powder with a pestle and mortar. Stir in the ground turmeric, Kashmiri chilli powder and 4 tbsp water to produce a thick paste. Set aside.

Bring a small saucepan of water to a boil, then add the quartered potatoes. Cook for 10-15 minutes, or until mostly cooked through. An inserted skewer should be met with a hint of resistance. Drain and set aside.

Heat the vegetable oil in a large saucepan over medium-high heat. Once hot, add the paste of fresh spices, stir for a minute, then reduce the heat and fry for 10 minutes, stirring, until it is fragrant, deeper in red and has split from the fat.

Add the paste of dry spices and lemongrass stalks. Fry for 2 minutes, then add the chicken, salt, caster sugar and light soy sauce. Reduce the heat, half-cover and let the chicken steam for 10 minutes, shaking the pan sporadically. Add the coconut milk. Bring to a robust simmer, then cover, lower the heat and simmer gently for 25 minutes.

Uncover, add the potatoes and simmer uncovered for another 15 minutes. By this point, both chicken and potatoes should be cooked to perfection. Add the coconut cream and curry leaves and cook for a final 3-4 minutes. Taste and adjust seasoning.

GULAI HOR CIO

At times I wonder if this dish's name was of my grandmother's coining: gulai is a Malay term referencing a spectrum of spicy braises, hor cio Hokkien for black pepper.

As a child, I never really did understand this dish. In comparison to the tamarind-laced braises and coconut-rich curries, this seemed lost and limp. It receded from memory, only bubbling up when I began researching Mon food in Myanmar, their soupy braises laced with a similar combination of spices. It was then that I began to appreciate its appeal, the magic of fresh spices left to their devices, their performance kept in check by both black pepper and belacan, their song untinted by acid.

The inclusion of soaked rice in the spice blend, according to my grandmother, was something she picked up from a Thai cook. A single teaspoon brings velvety smoothness to the liquid without loosening its profile. My grandmother would boil the liquefied rempah for hours to expel any fishiness before adding the meat. I find an hour sufficient. And although I do not make the yardlong beans as swollen and slithery as she did, you want them soft and drunk on flavour.

SERVES 6-8

1 tsp jasmine rice
1 tbsp black peppercorns
4 garlic cloves, peeled
5 shallots (approx. 30g), peeled
100g red chillies, sliced
2 lemongrass stalks, tender portion only, sliced
15g ginger, peeled and sliced
20g turmeric, peeled and sliced
20g galangal, peeled and sliced
8 makrut lime leaves
30g fermented shrimp paste (*belacan*), toasted (page 219)
1 litre water
1 tsp caster sugar
1 tsp salt
1.4kg chicken, jointed into 8
200g yardlong beans, cut into 7cm sections

Soak the jasmine rice in a small bowl of water for 1 hour.

Toast the black peppercorns in a dry frying pan over medium-low heat until fragrant.

Drain the rice and put it, with the black pepper, into the goblet of a liquidiser. Add the garlic, shallots, red chillies, lemongrass, ginger, turmeric, galangal, 4 of the makrut lime leaves, toasted fermented shrimp paste and water, blend into a smooth liquid and tip into a saucepan. (Alternatively, pound everything with a pestle and mortar, scoop the resultant paste into the saucepan and add the water.) Add the caster sugar and salt and place over medium-high heat. Bring to a boil for 2 minutes, then turn the heat down to its lowest setting, cover and simmer gently for 1 hour.

Add the jointed chicken, cover again and simmer for 30-40 minutes or until just tender. Add the yardlong bean sections and rip in the remaining 4 makrut lime leaves. Simmer for another 7-10 minutes, without a lid or until the beans are soft. This has to be enjoyed with plenty of hot rice.

GULAI KEO

As with the previous entry, the name of this dish is a Malay–Hokkien hybrid: keo is Hokkien for eggplant.

The fried salted threadfin bones add umami to the sauce, bringing to mind sun-baked beaches and salt on the lips, but without harshing its mellow. In place of this, a handful of medium shrimp, freed of heads and armours, may be added towards the end of the cooking time.

SERVES 6

250g salted threadfin bones

for the spice paste
5 garlic cloves, peeled
50g shallots, peeled weight
20g ginger, peeled and sliced
10g turmeric, peeled
1 red chilli, deseeded and sliced
4 bird's eye chillies
2 dried chillies, deseeded and
    softened (page 218)
1 tsp fermented shrimp paste
    (*belacan*), toasted (page 219)

for the dry spice blend
1 tbsp coriander seeds
1½ tsp fennel seeds
½ tsp ground fenugreek

to cook
1 tsp caster sugar
1 tsp coconut sugar (*gula melaka*)
1 tsp salt
600ml coconut milk
750g Chinese eggplants
2 green chillies, slit lengthwise
15 curry leaves
100ml coconut cream
Vegetable oil, for frying

Begin the night before. Place the salted threadfin bones in a bowl and rinse in several changes of water to remove surfeit salt. Immerse the bones in a generous amount of fresh water, cover and leave in a cool place overnight.

The following day, drain the soaked threadfin bones in a sieve or colander. Give them a rinse under a running tap and leave them to drip dry. Meanwhile, make the spice paste by pounding the necessary ingredients together with a pestle and mortar or in a cosy blender with a tiny bit of water. Set aside.

Lightly toast the coriander and fennel seeds in a small frying pan over medium heat. Once aromatic and lightly coloured, tip into a pestle and mortar and pound into a powder. Tip into a bowl, mix in the ground fenugreek and add 2 tbsp water to form a loose paste. Set that aside as well.

Fill a wok or wide saucepan with approximately 4cm of vegetable oil. Place over medium heat. Once hot but not smoking, add the drained salted threadfin bones and fry to a golden turn. They will begin to smell quite appetising. Drain and set aside momentarily.

Decant and discard all the oil in the wok. Give the pan a wipe, place it over medium-high heat, then add 100ml fresh vegetable oil. Once hot, add the spice paste. Fry for a minute, stirring constantly, then lower the heat and fry for 10-12 minutes or until it deepens in colour and releases warming aromas.

Scrape in the paste of dry spices, fry for a minute to drive out its rawness, then add the caster sugar, coconut sugar, salt, coconut milk and the fried fish bones. Raise the heat and allow it to boil for a minute. Then lower the heat, cover and simmer gently for 20 minutes.

Meanwhile, run a vegetable peeler along the lengths of the eggplants at 1cm intervals. Cut the striped fruit into 7cm sections, then cut these into quarters.

When the *gulai* has had its 20 minutes, add the prepared eggplant and simmer, half-covered, for 5 minutes. Now stir in the green chillies, curry leaves and coconut cream. Simmer, this time without a lid, for 7 minutes, just so it thickens a little. The finished sauce should have the consistency of double cream.

SAMBAL TELUR IKAN BILIS

Every Hari Raya, my mother's company driver would give us nasi minyak, sayur lodeh, ayam masak merah, rendang, lontong, and this, essentially boiled eggs, firm tofu and crisp-fried dried anchovies bound in a rich, spicy sauce.

You may add a couple of bird's eye chillies to the spice paste if a more intense heat is preferred.

SERVES 4-6

for the spice paste
2 garlic cloves, peeled
75g shallots, peeled
225g red chillies, sliced
2 tsp fermented shrimp paste
    (*belacan*), toasted (page 219)

to cook
50g dried anchovies, washed and dried
    (page 218)
5 hardboiled eggs, peeled
300g firm beancurd
    (*tau kwa*), quartered
1 medium red onion, peeled and sliced
50ml water
2½ tsp caster sugar
A pinch or so salt
Vegetable oil, for frying

Make the spice paste by pounding the ingredients with a pestle and mortar until fine. Alternatively, blitz them in a cosy blender, adding a teeny bit of water to help them along if necessary.

Heat about 1½cm vegetable oil in a wide saucepan or deep frying pan over medium heat. Add the dried anchovies and fry, stirring, until they are golden and crisp. Tip out onto a plate lined with kitchen towel.

In the same oil, fry the hardboiled eggs and *tau kwa* separately to seal them. The odd touch of brown is welcome. Convey these to another plate lined with kitchen towel.

Discard the oil in the pan. Give the pan a brief wipe, then pour in another 100ml vegetable oil and place over medium heat. Once hot, add the spice paste, stir for a minute, then lower the heat slightly and cook, stirring, until it splits in the oil and has turned a rich carmine.

Stir in the sliced red onion, water, caster sugar, salt, fried beancurd and eggs. Simmer over a lowish heat for 5-7 minutes, until the sauce has thickened to coat the eggs and beancurd. Stir in the crisp-fried anchovies. A final 30 seconds and the dish is done.

CHAI BUEY 菜尾

Chai buey, in Hokkien, simply means "leftovers", the chief component of this dish, commonly prepared after special occasions to eke out, and expand on, leftovers from wedding, birthday and Lunar New Year celebrations — in particular cuts of roasted chicken, duck or pork.

While the meat adds body and umami, it is the tua chai, dai gai choy or large-petiole mustard (Brassica juncea integrifolia strumata) that steals the show with its generous, succulent leaves and gorgeous, mid-toned bitterness. Some recipes use kiam chai, essentially the same vegetable preserved with salt.

Tartness is an important feature in chai buey. My souring agents of choice are tomatoes and asam keping, which are dried slices of asam gelugur (Garcinia atroviridis). You may use tamarind water if the latter eludes you.

SERVES 6

500g large-petiole mustard
2 tbsp vegetable oil
4 garlic cloves, peeled and crushed
2 medium red onions, peeled and sliced
2 tomatoes, quartered
1 lemongrass stalk, bruised
400g roast pork belly, cut up
　　(page 207)
½ tsp white peppercorns, toasted
　　and crushed
2 tsp light soy sauce
½ tsp dark soy sauce
1 litre chicken stock (page 221)
6 pieces *asam keping*
6 dried chillies, softened
　　(page 218)
Salt, sugar

Inspect the large-petiole mustard, removing any outer leaves that are bruised or wilted. Then dismantle it, cutting the larger leaves into halves or quarters, leaving the smaller ones whole.

Bring a large saucepan of water to a boil over high heat, then add the prepared mustard leaves. Blanch for 2 minutes, then drain in a colander. Give the leaves a wash under a cold tap, then shake off excess liquid. Set aside.

Dry the recently used saucepan and return it to the stove, over medium-high heat. Add the vegetable oil, and once it heats up, add the garlic. Fry until pale gold and fragrant, then add the red onions. Once they have softened slightly and adopted some colour, add the tomatoes, lemongrass, roast pork belly and white peppercorns. Lower the heat and fry for 5 minutes, stirring.

Add the light and dark soy sauces, followed by the chicken stock, *asam keping* and dried chillies. There should be enough liquid to barely cover the meat. Cover and simmer for 20 minutes. Uncover the pot and add the blanched greens. Reinstate the lid and simmer for another 30 minutes or until the mustard leaves are deliciously soft. Taste and tweak with salt and sugar.

STEAMED EGG CUSTARD 蒸水蛋

Most Chinese households make some kind of steamed egg custard. This version features minced pork and dong cai, a Tianjin speciality of chopped cabbage preserved in salt, commonly sold in small packets.

To achieve a smooth custard, it is essential to avoid overwhisking the eggs and to spoon off any bubbles besmirching its surface. It is also vital to steam the custard over the gentlest possible heat and in a tray with small perforations.

SERVES 4-6

3 tbsp *dong cai*
75g pork mince
A dash of white pepper
¼ tsp cornflour
Few drops of toasted sesame oil
3 eggs
Two pinches of salt
Water

to serve
2 spring onions, finely sliced
2 tbsp crisp-fried shallots (page 220)

Prepare your steamer.

Place the *dong cai* in a small bowl and rinse 3-4 times to remove surfeit salt. Cover it in 2cm of fresh water and let it steep for 10 minutes. Have a little taste: its saltiness, while pronounced, should not be piercing. Drain and set aside.

In a separate bowl, gently combine the pork mince, white pepper, cornflour and toasted sesame seed oil, then stir in half the *dong cai*. Tip this mixture into a heatproof dish 500ml in capacity and 4cm in depth, spreading it evenly over its base.

Crack the eggs into a measuring jug and gently whisk to combine. Thin it with 1½ times its volume in water, sprinkle in the salt and whisk until well-mixed. Any froth or bubbles may be removed with a spoon. Strain this over the contents in the heatproof bowl. Sprinkle over the remaining *dong cai*.

Gingerly convey this to the belly of the steamer. Cover and steam over the lowest possible heat until smoothly set, about 35-40 minutes. A modicum of wobble should be detected.

Remove it from the steamer very carefully, then shower with finely sliced spring onions and crisp-fried shallots.

SAMBAL PETAI UDANG

This is something with which all Singaporeans, Malaysians, Thais and Indonesians would be familiar: stink beans fried with a red balm of crushed spices and shrimp.

Some cooks prefer this more richly sauced, but I like a snug fit. I also like the petai to pack a modicum of bite.

SERVES 4

for the spice paste
4 garlic cloves, peeled
25g shallots, peeled weight
10g ginger, peeled and sliced
50g red chillies, deseeded
3 dried chillies, deseeded and
    softened (page 218)
1 tsp fermented shrimp paste
    (*belacan*), toasted (page 219)
15g dried shrimp, softened (page 219)

to cook
125g stink beans (*petai*)
125g medium prawns, peeled weight
5 tbsp vegetable oil
2 tsp caster sugar
¼ tsp salt
1 tbsp tamarind water (page 221)
4 tbsp water

Make the spice paste by pounding the ingredients together with a pestle and mortar or in a cosy blender with a tiny bit of water.

With a small paring knife, prise the stink beans into halves and devein the prawns.

In a wok or deep frying pan, heat the vegetable oil over medium-high heat. Once hot, add the spice paste, fry for about a minute, stirring constantly. Then turn the heat down to medium-low and fry for 10-12 minutes, or until the paste is deep red and has split from the oil.

Stir in the prawns. Just as they turn opaque and curl up, add the stink beans, caster sugar, salt, tamarind water and water. Cook, stirring gently, until the stink beans are tender crisp, about 2-3 minutes.

MEE SIAM GORENG

Both my grandmother and mother taught one of our Filipino helpers how to make this. Though not an intuitive cook, she was curious, keen and tenacious, and this became one of her signatures that she would proudly make whenever there were large gatherings at home.

The exact dimensions of the 100g block of firm tofu are not salient; you just want most of the cubes encrusted for contrast.

Not everyone shares my penchant for raw beansprouts and garlic chives. If you fall in this camp, simply toss them into the noodles in their last minute on the stove.

SERVES 4-6

200g rice vermicelli (*bee hoon*)
8 tbsp vegetable oil
100g block firm tofu (*tau kwa*)
1 large egg
1 tbsp salted fermented soy beans (*taucheo*), crushed into a paste
1 tsp caster sugar, plus more to taste
1 tbsp tamarind water (page 221)
150g medium prawns, peeled weight, deveined
75ml chicken stock (page 221) or anchovy stock (page 218)
A few drops dark soy sauce
Salt, to taste

for the spice paste
4 garlic cloves, peeled
75g shallots, peeled
50g red chillies, sliced
4 dried chillies, softened (page 218)
2 candlenuts
25g dried shrimps, softened (page 219)
½ tsp fermented shrimp paste, toasted (page 219)

to finish
100g beansprouts
4 garlic chives, cut into 3cm sections
4 red bird's eye chillies, thinly sliced on a diagonal
Calamansi limes, halved

Soak the rice vermicelli in a bowl of boiling water for 10 minutes or until just pliable. Drain and set aside.

Heat 1 tbsp of the vegetable in a 22cm frying pan. (This dimension is only important for the omelette that you will be frying shortly.) Pat the firm tofu dry with kitchen towel and brown it on all sides in the hot fat. Remove to a plate.

Add 1 tbsp more oil to the pan. Whisk the egg with a pinch of salt and caster sugar, then pour it into the pan, swirling to create a thin omelette. Once its underside is set and faintly brown, flip it and cook the other side to the same effect. Convey the omelette to a chopping board and leave to cool.

Cut the fried firm tofu into 1½cm squares on its plate. Tightly roll the cooled omelette and cut it into ½cm ribbons.

Make the spice paste by pounding the ingredients together with a pestle and mortar or in a cosy blender with a tiny bit of water.

In a wok or deep frying pan, heat the remaining 6 tbsp vegetable oil over medium-high heat. Once hot, add the spice paste, fry for about a minute, stirring constantly. Then turn the heat down to medium-low and fry for 12-15 minutes, or until the paste is deeper in red and has split in the oil.

Add the *tau cheo*, fry for a minute, stirring constantly, then add the caster sugar and tamarind water. Stir until the sugar dissolves into the paste. Stir in the prawns, then the stock and dark soy sauce.

Once the prawns curl and the liquid bubbles, add the soaked rice vermicelli, turning it over so that it drinks up all the spice-tinted liquid, softening further in the process. The vermicelli should be tender and springy, not *al dente*, so add a dash more stock (or water) if need be. Do not go overboard as the noodles go soggy easily. Taste and adjust seasoning.

Convey the *mee siam* to a platter, spreading the noodles out across its surface. Scatter with the cubed *tau kwa* and sliced omelette, raw beansprouts, garlic chives and red bird's eye chillies. Serve with a bowl bearing the halved calamansi limes.

LAKSA LEMAK

The mineraliness of the cockles provides a welcome counterpoint to the richness of the coconut-laced gravy. The recipe beneath assumes you are going to be using these freshly gouged out from their salt-and-pepper ridged shells. If this task gives you anxiety, then it may be helpful to note that Asian fishmongers often sell cockle flesh in packets, though their essence can seem somewhat diluted.

For the attendant photograph, I snipped the noodles into short sections and served bowlfuls with spoons, as is done by some hawkers. You may, of course, keep the strands intact.

SERVES 6

for the spice paste
5 garlic cloves, peeled
75g shallots, peeled weight
15g ginger, peeled and sliced
25g galangal, peeled and sliced
15g turmeric, peeled and sliced
25g red chillies, sliced
4 dried chillies, deseeded and soaked
   (page 218)
2 red bird's eye chillies
2 lemongrass stalks, tender portions
   only, sliced
3 candlenuts
2 tsp fermented shrimp paste
   (*belacan*), toasted (page 219)

for the broth
65g dried shrimp
2 tsp coriander seeds
75ml vegetable oil
600ml prawn stock (page 221)
600ml coconut milk (page 218)
1 tsp salt, plus more to taste
1 tsp caster sugar, plus more to taste
150ml coconut cream
30g tofu puffs (*tau pok*), cut into
   ½cm slices
A stalk of Vietnamese mint
   (laksa leaves)

Make the spice paste by pounding the ingredients together with a pestle and mortar or whizzing in a cosy blender with a tiny bit of water. Set aside.

Soak the dried shrimp in a bowl of cold water for 10 minutes. Drain well and pound with a pestle and mortar or blitz in a cosy blender into an airy floss. Set aside.

Toast the coriander seeds in a small frying pan over medium-low heat until they release their aromas and acquire a hint of colour. Tip into a pestle and mortar, cool for a few minutes, then crush into a fine powder. Scrape out in a small bowl and set aside.

Heat the vegetable oil in a large saucepan over medium heat. Add the spice paste, stir, then reduce the heat to medium-low and fry for 15-20 minutes, stirring constantly, until the paste deepens in colour, turning a deep ochre, and splits in the oil. Sprinkle in the pounded dried shrimp and fry until fragrant, 5-7 minutes.

Stir in the ground toasted coriander seeds and cook for 30 seconds. Add the prawn stock, coconut milk, salt and caster sugar. Once it bubbles, cover, reduce the heat and simmer gently for 45 minutes.

Use this time to tend to the remaining ingredients. Blanch the fresh rice vermicelli as per packet instructions; it usually takes no longer than a minute. Drain in a sieve, refresh under cold water, shake to dry, then tip into a large basin or bowl.

500g fresh thick rice vermicelli
    (laksa noodles)
300g medium prawns
50g fried Chinese fish cakes
125g beansprouts
50g blood cockles, *optional*
Leaves from a bunch of Vietnamese
    mint (laksa leaves), finely chopped
Calamansi limes, halved

Poach the prawns in a saucepan of simmering water, just until they curl up and turn bright orange. Cool, peel and halve, removing dark threads of innards.

Soak the fish cakes in warm water for 1-2 minutes, to remove the slime that comes with being cooped up in a packet in the fridge, then drain and cut into slivers.

Pick over the beansprouts, removing any black or wizened bits. If you are using blood cockles, immerse the bivalves in a bowl of hot water for 5 minutes, then drain and prise them open.

Finely chop the Vietnamese mint, halve the calamansi limes.

When the soup has had its 45 minutes, add the coconut cream, *tau pok* and the stalk of Vietnamese mint. Let it simmer on low heat for just 5 minutes, then taste and adjust seasoning with salt and sugar.

Divide the rice noodles among 6 bowls and adorn each mound with the poached shrimp, slivered fish cakes, fresh beansprouts and cockles. Finally, ladle the broth over. Sprinkle with chopped Vietnamese mint leaves and serve with calamansi limes.

HAE MEE

The broth for the prawn noodles of Penang (also referred to there as Hokkien mee) is different than its Singapore counterpart on two counts. One, it is usually devoid of, or very shy with, whole spices, such as star anise and clove, and second, it has some of the accompanying sambal cooked into it, which imparts a pleasing shade of crimson.

Some cooks add both dried and fresh prawns to their broth, but I only use the latter. Medium-sized ones, from the sea and not the farm, work the best. If you find, for whatever reason, the prawn flavour a trifle overpowering, a blade of pandan, warmed over a burner and dropped into the pot, will come to your aid.

Prawns are only part of the equation here: pork is also present. There are some who enjoy making a proper porcine feast out of this, adding pig's tails and small intenstines to the party. In our family, we usually just use pork ribs. Occasionally, we remove the ribs from the broth and eat them separately from the noodles, with chilli powder and plum sauce, sometimes calamansi lime juice and coriander.

As for the all-important carbohydrate, I like a combination of fresh yellow egg noodles and boiled rice vermicelli (bee hoon) here. Some prefer having only either. Others prefer flat rice noodles (kway teow) instead.

SERVES 6

for the stock
1kg pork ribs
400g chicken carcass
2 litres water
1½ tsp salt
1 tsp light soy sauce
2 tbsp Shaoxing rice wine
1 tsp white peppercorns
3 garlic cloves

for the prawns
2kg medium prawns

for the sambal
6 garlic cloves, peeled
100g shallots, peeled weight
20 dried chillies, approx. 25g,
    deseeded and softened (page 218)
2 tsp fermented shrimp paste
    (*belacan*), toasted (page 219)
5 tbsp vegetable oil
2 tsp caster sugar
Salt

to cook
3 tbsp vegetable oil
4 garlic cloves, peeled and bruised
1 tsp light soy sauce
2 tsp dark soy sauce
1 tsp fish sauce
10g rock sugar
Vegetable oil, for frying

to serve
500g fresh egg noodles
150g dried rice vermicelli, blanched
200g water convolvulus, cut into
    4cm sections
125g beansprouts
Crisp-fried shallots (page 220)
Chilli powder
Plum sauce

Begin with the stock. Scald the pork ribs in a pot of boiling water for 5 minutes, then strain and return to the pot with the remaining ingredients. Bring to a vigorous boil for 2-3 minutes, then reduce the heat, cover and simmer gently for 2 hours.

Meanwhile, peel the prawns, removing their heads and shells, but not their tails. You require approx. 1kg of shells and heads. Of the peeled prawns, you only require 300g; the rest may be frozen and kept for other purposes. Refrigerate the shells, heads and flesh of the prawns until needed.

Make the *sambal*. Pound the garlic, shallots, softened dried chillies and toasted fermented shrimp paste together or blitz them in a cosy blender with a tiny bit of water.

Heat the vegetable oil in a deep frying pan over medium-high heat. Once hot, add the spice paste. Fry for a minute, stirring furiously, then reduce the heat and cook until you get an oily, rich red paste. Stir in the caster sugar, cook for just a further minute, then turn off the heat. Taste and season with salt. You will require half of this *sambal* for the broth, the remaining half for serving with the noodles.

When the stock has had its 2 hours, tong out the pork ribs and set aside. Strain the stock through a fine mesh sieve. You want approximately 1¼ litres. Reserve the pork ribs.

Remove the peeled prawns and the bowl of heads and shells from the cold.

Give the stock pot a wash and wipe, then return it over medium heat. Add the oil, which should heat up in no time, then the prawn shells and heads and bruised garlic. Fry, stirring constantly, until the shells and heads are red and the garlic is golden. Pour in the stock and bring it to a boil. Turn the heat down to its lowest, cover and simmer for 25 minutes. Cool slightly, then blend in a liquidiser and strain back into the pot through a fine mesh sieve, crushing it through best as you can.

Bring the pot of prawn stock to a boil over high heat. Add half the *sambal*, light and dark soy sauces, fish sauce and rock sugar. Cover and simmer for 20-25 minutes. Taste and adjust seasoning. Add the peeled prawns and cooked pork ribs to the pot. Simmer for 5 minutes, until the prawns are cooked. Reduce the heat to its lowest setting, cover and let the stock gently putter.

Blanch the egg noodles and rice vermicelli separately, as well as the water convolvulus and beansprouts. Divide among 4 large bowls.

Bring the stock to a rolling boil once again and ladle it over the noodles, ensuring each bowl has some prawns and pork ribs. Sprinkle with crisp-fried shallots and serve alongside little bowls of the remaining *sambal* to go with the noodles, and also chilli powder and plum sauce to accompany the pork ribs.

MEE SUA TNG 面线汤

*In the past, mee sua, wheat vermicelli, would have to be washed to remove surfeit starch.
These days, with improved levels of manufacturing, this step may be omitted.*

*The dried shrimp gives the soup body and it is crucial that you fry it until
warmingly fragrant.*

I use nai bai cai here, dwarf bok choy, but any Chinese green would work.

SERVES 2

50g dried shrimp
4 garlic cloves, peeled
1 tsp white peppercorns
4 tbsp vegetable oil
1¼ litres pork stock (page 221)
150g wheat vermicelli (*mee sua*)
75g dwarf bok choy (*nai bai cai*)
2 eggs
Salt and light soy sauce, to taste
2 spring onions, finely sliced

Rinse the dried shrimp under a running tap, then soak in a bowl of
cold water for 10 minutes. Drain well and pound with a mortar and
pestle into a floss. Tip this out into a bowl and use the pestle and
mortar to pound the garlic and white peppercorns into a paste.

Heat the vegetable oil in a large saucepan over medium-high heat.
Once hot, add the garlic-white peppercorn paste. Fry until lightly
coloured and fragrant, stirring constantly. Add the dried shrimp floss
and fry until reddish and fragrant. Pour in the pork stock, bring to a
boil, then cover and turn the heat down to its lowest setting. Simmer
for 15 minutes.

Uncover the pot and raise the heat so the broth boils. Add the wheat
vermicelli and stir to prevent them from sticking. Once the strands
are just tender, add the greens and crack in the eggs. Reduce the heat
slightly and allow the eggs to poach in the simmering liquid. I like
wisps of white and waxy, slightly molten yolks, so this seldom takes
more than a minute. Turn off the heat. Season to taste with salt. You
may add a few drops of light soy sauce, but exercise restraint.

Divide between 2 generous soup bowls. Sprinkle with spring onions
and eat.

WATERMELON MASAK TITEK

The full name for this dish featuring watermelon rind, popular among Penang Peranakans, is xi gua masak titek and how it earned it remains unclear; titek or titik means "to point" or "to drop". Coming from an austere period, my grandmother would flavour this just with dried shrimp and use wintermelon or bottle gourd.

This recipe uses fresh prawns, crushed into a paste and dropped into the soup where it sets into free-form dumplings, as well as fermented shrimp paste. I add a dash of untraditional fish sauce for a sweeter savouriness.

SERVES 4-6

500g medium prawns
1 litre water
½ tsp white peppercorns
4 shallots, peeled and sliced
½ tsp fermented shrimp paste
    (*belacan*), toasted (page 219)
1 tsp fish sauce
1kg watermelon segments
4 red bird's eye chillies,
    lightly crushed
Salt, to taste
Vegetable oil, for frying

Separate the prawn shells and heads from their flesh. You require just 150g flesh; the rest may be kept for other uses.

Fry the prawn shells and heads with 1 tbsp vegetable oil in a medium saucepan over medium heat, just until orange. Add the water. Bring to a boil, cover and simmer for 25 minutes. Strain into a heatproof jug.

Toast the white peppercorns in a dry frying pan until fragrant, then finely pound with 2 of the shallots and fermented shrimp paste with a pestle and mortar. Remove this to a bowl.

To the mortar, add the 150g peeled prawn flesh from earlier, the remaining 2 shallots and fish sauce and pound into a sticky grey paste. Set this paste aside.

Peel the green skin off the watermelon segments, then slice off all but ½cm of the rubied flesh from their pale jade rind. Eat the removed flesh while you cut the two-toned rind segments into 2cm pieces. You should get approx. 500g. Set aside.

Heat 1 tbsp vegetable oil in a medium saucepan over medium heat. Add the shallot-white pepper paste, stir, then reduce the heat and fry until fragrant, 2-3 minutes. Add the prawn stock and bring to a boil. Add the prepared watermelon rind and red bird's eye chillies. Cover, reduce the heat, and simmer for 10-12 minutes or until the melon rind is tender while retaining a little crispness.

Uncover, drop in teaspoonfuls of the prawn mixture and cook for 1-2 minutes or until opaque. Taste and tweak with salt.

LOTUS ROOT SOUP 莲藕汤

Most Chinese families would have a double boiler in which to make soup, the mild, indirect heat preserving delicate flavours and nutrients. All one has to do is bung in the ingredients and press the start button. In our home the contraption would be filled with broths crayoned with corn, bulked with watercress and jujubes, and chunks of lotus root. This recipe, however, is designed for the stove.

This soup tastes much better the following day, after the ingredients have had some quiet time to mingle without pressure. Dried cuttlefish and tablets of dried scallops may be added to the pot for a greater hit of umami.

SERVES 6

75g raw unskinned peanuts
750g pork ribs, cut into 4cm pieces
500g lotus root, peeled and cut into
    1cm slices
2 garlic cloves, unpeeled
4 honey or red dates
2 tsp salt, plus more to taste
1 tsp light soy sauce
2 litres water
A few drops dark soy sauce, *optional*

Soak the peanuts in a bowl of water for 1 hour, then drain.

Fill a medium saucepan with water and bring to a boil over high heat. Add the pork ribs and blanch for 5 minutes, then drain in a colander and wash well.

Put the blanched ribs into a larger saucepan with the lotus root, garlic, honey or red dates, salt, light soy sauce, water, soaked peanuts and a few drops of dark soy sauce if you want a richer colour.

Bring to a boil over high heat for a minute, then reduce the heat, cover and simmer for 1½-2 hours or until the meat is tender. You could leave it up to 2½-3 hours if you prefer; the meat may fall off the bone, but the soup will taste more intense. Taste and season with salt. As mentioned above, this soup comes into its own the following day.

MUAH CHEE 麻糍

These days, many recipes for this soft, glutinous rice cake, involve steamers. This one uses a frying pan. It demands patience and elbow grease, but the aroma exuded by the glutinous pastry as it sizzles and swells in hot fat, even catching in parts, makes it all worthwhile. The oil in question, however, has to be infused with fried shallots. It is a delight for both the palate and olfaction, one my mother associates with the muah chee of her childhood. Most cooks discard the allium filings after they have performed their task. I, however, prefer them to participate in the eating experience and so add them to the rubble of sweetened peanuts and sesame (I use both black and white).

SERVES 6-8

for the batter
150g glutinous rice flour
10g tapioca starch
Pinch of salt
1 tsp caster sugar
250ml water
6 tbsp vegetable oil
4 shallots, peeled and thinly sliced

for the topping
100g roasted peanuts (page 220),
    finely chopped
3 tbsp toasted white sesame seeds
    (page 220), lightly crushed
3 tbsp toasted black sesame seeds
    (page 220), lightly crushed
75g caster sugar
Pinch of salt

for cooking
6 tbsp vegetable oil
4 shallots, peeled and thinly sliced

Combine the glutinous rice flour, tapioca starch, salt and caster sugar in a bowl. Whisk in the water to get a smooth batter.

Combine the peanuts, black and white sesame seeds, caster sugar and salt in a large shallow dish. Cover and keep in a cool place until required.

In a wide saucepan, heat the vegetable oil over medium heat. Once hot, add the shallots and fry, stirring, until crisp and golden, lowering the flame slightly midway. Remove the crisp-fried shallots with a slotted spoon to the dish of sweetened peanuts and sesame. Decant off some of the oil so that you only have 3 tbsp left in the pan. (Reserve the decanted oil for future use, despite the rather measly quantity.)

Return the pan to the stove, this time over medium-low heat. Pour in the glutinous rice batter. Stir immediately and continuously with a wooden spoon or heatproof spatula until you get a thick, smooth, blubber-like mass. Reduce the heat to its lowest and continue cooking this mass, pressing it against the hot metal, flipping and swirling until it is glossy, fat quietly sizzling around its edges. It should also have swollen slightly, attaining a new bounciness and a hint of translucence, and no longer smell raw.

Tip the *muah chee* out onto a tray. Leave to cool a little, then cut with a pair of scissors, an oiled knife or a pastry cutter into morsels and roll these in the sweetened, shallot-peanut-sesame mixture.

○ KU KUEH

Most people are familiar with ang ku kueh, a glutinous rice pastry stuffed with crushed, lightly sweetened mung beans, tinted and moulded to resemble, as its name suggests, a red tortoise. This is its black counterpart, traditionally reserved for special occasions, like Ching Ming and the Hungry Ghost Festival. It is not so easy to find these days, as the leaves required for its herbal inkiness have become elusive, at least in Singapore. These include ramie leaves (Boehmeria nivea), cudweed (Gnaphalium affine), skunkvine (Paederia foetida) and Chinese mugwort (Artemisia argyi). For this recipe, dried ramie leaves have been employed.

It is essential to remove the central veins from the dried leaves as they are resilient, even surviving bullet blenders, speckling the finished product. It is also important to boil the prepared leaves with alkaline water. More than producing a sterner shade of black, it also seems to help break down the leaf fibres.

Now, this recipe is a mischievous one, demanding you make far more ramie purée than is needed. Almost double, in fact. The reason is that cooking a smaller amount of leaves will require a tiny saucepan and very timid flames; the risk of all the water evaporating would otherwise be raised. I did not increase the recipe's yield as the kueh do not keep and frankly my family seldom sees an occasion that requires more than a dozen. The good news is that the ramie purée freezes like a dream.

MAKES 14

for the ramie paste
20g dried *ramie* leaves
600ml water
¼ tsp alkaline water

for the pastry
100g glutinous rice flour
60g yellow-fleshed sweet potato,
    peeled weight, cut into 2cm chunks
1 tsp rice flour
1 tsp caster sugar
¼ tsp salt
1½ tsp vegetable oil
Fourteen 7cm banana leaf squares,
    unsoftened

Begin one day before you wish to make the actual *kueh*.

First, make the *ramie* paste. Pick over the dried *ramie* leaves, removing the central veins. Place the tidied leaves in a sieve and give them a quick rinse under a cold tap. Squeeze these leaves into a ball, then place in a medium saucepan with the water and alkaline water. Bring to a boil over high heat, then turn the heat down to its lowest, cover and simmer for 45 minutes or until very soft, stirring occasionally, until most of the liquid has either been absorbed or evaporated.

Cool the mixture and blend into a thick, smooth purée. You should get 200-250g, depending on the thirst of the dried leaves. Measure out 125g and keep the rest for future use in an air-tight container in the fridge for up to 3 days and in the freezer for up to 2 weeks.

for the filling
125g split peeled mung beans
    (*moong dal*)
90ml vegetable oil
2 shallots, peeled and thinly sliced
75g caster sugar
¼ tsp salt

In a bowl, combine the glutinous rice flour for the pastry with 75g *ramie* purée. The resultant mixture should be ashen and crumbly, like damp volcanic soil. Cover and refrigerate for 8-12 hours or overnight. (The remaining 50g *ramie* purée should also be refrigerated.)

The *ramie*-dampened flour will not be sleeping alone: pick over and rinse the *moong dal*, then soak in a bowl of water overnight.

Begin the following day by cooking the filling. Prepare a steamer, filling its lower compartment with plenty of water and lining its perforated compartment with muslin. Drain the *moong dal*, spread them over the muslin and steam over medium-high heat for 30 minutes or until fluffy and tender. The cooked *dal* should disintegrate when lightly pressed between fingers. Tip them out into a bowl but do not wash the steamer yet.

Heat the vegetable oil in a large saucepan or wok over medium heat. Add the shallots, lower the heat slightly and fry until golden and fragrant, about 5 minutes. Discard all the shallots – they have done their work – and leave 4 tbsp of the infused oil in the pan. Do not discard the removed oil; it has a role to fulfill. Stir in the mung beans and fry, crushing them into the oil. Add the caster sugar and salt and continue cooking until a soft, smooth paste, like mashed potato, is obtained. This paste will stiffen upon cooling. Transfer to a bowl and cool completely.

Now, finish the pastry. Boil the chunked sweet potato in a little water in a small saucepan until tender, then drain and crush into a balm in a large mixing bowl. Give the saucepan a rinse, then into it place the rice flour, remaining 50g *ramie* purée, caster sugar, salt and oil. Place this saucepan over medium-low heat, whisking and cooking its contents into an inky, oleaginous paste. Scrape this over the crushed sweet potatoes, stir it in well, then leave to cool completely.

Once the sweet potato mixture has cooled, tip in the *ramie*-soaked glutinous rice flour and massage the lot into a smooth dough, adding a tiny bit of water if necessary. Cover and leave for 30 minutes, then divide the dough into 14 balls, arranging them on a tray and covering with a damp tea towel to prevent them from drying out.

Meanwhile, divide the sweet mung bean paste into 14 balls and, as with the pastry, arrange these on a (separate) tray and cover with a damp tea towel.

At last, the fun bit has arrived. Lightly dust your work surface with glutinous rice flour. Do the same for the interiors of the *kueh ku* mould, rapping to expel any excess. Lightly oil the banana leaf squares with some of the reserved shallot oil.

In between lightly floured palms, flatten a ball of dough into a 6cm disc, then pop a portion of bean filling in the middle. Bring the sides of the pastry over the filling, pinch to conceal, then roll this parcel into a ball. Dust with a little glutinous rice flour, then press it firmly into the mould with your palm. Strike the handle of the mould against your work surface, thereby freeing the *kueh*. Arrange this on an oiled banana leaf square and lower this into a perforated steamer compartment. Continue making all the *o ku kueh* this way.

Top up the water in the lower compartment of the steamer and place it over high heat. Once the water is boiling, place on the *kueh*-filled compartment, reduce the heat and steam for 7-9 minutes, until the skins of the *kueh* have turned supple and deepened in blackness.

Remove the compartment from the steamer vessel, uncover it and let the *kueh* cool for 2 minutes before anointing with a little of the reserved shallot oil. (If you brush them immediately, you risk marring their beautiful, patterned countenances.) You may trim off the excess leaf around the pastries, but I seldom bother.

These are best consumed on their day of birth. Leftovers may be stowed in an airtight container in the refrigerator for a day or so, but are seldom as delectable even after being reheated. You could consider, however, frying them in a lightly oiled pan until crusty without and warm and squidgy within.

OVALS

One thing I associate with my paternal grandmother is her fondness for the snake plant, whose wicked tips she would conceal with vacated egg shells. The yellow-rimmed, oval-capped blades occupied most of the front and back lawns for as long as I can remember. Pots of them fringed the veranda. Some even found homes in clay urns once used for brewing soy sauce.

Ill-equipped to handle Teochew and Mandarin, exchanges between us were often short and sweet, dissolving quicker than haw tablets on the tongue, the ballooning silence pricked by the timely appearance of lacquer salvers bearing pumpkin and melon seeds, White Rabbit milk candies and Kopiko coffee sweets.

Meals rarely occurred at her house. When they did, the food would be unfussy and cosy. Steamed pomfret with sour plums and tomatoes. A boiled pork belly, carved and dressed with soy, chillies and garlic. Pork ribs braised with bittergourd and salted fermented black beans. *Mangkuang kueh* and *ku chai kueh* from reliable suppliers, their cargoes of jicama and garlic chives threatening to rupture the dumplings' clammy, translucent skins.

The bulk of our eating sessions took place in restaurants, mostly Teochew ones, the food a trifle more elaborate. Fine slices of soy-braised duck and quaking tiles of tofu. Golden, frilly-edged omelettes punctuated with oysters no larger than dollar coins. Steamed blueswimmers, their flesh, soft as apple blossoms, dripped with black vinegar. Storm clouds of *orh nee*, crushed taro yam cooked for a loving number of hours with lard and sugar, interrupted by the odd jewel of gingko.

PNG KUEH 潮州饭粿

I used to find these peach-shaped cakes stultifying and bland, and would observe my father snaffling platefuls for supper after work in both awe and horror. I have since learned that cooking the glutinous rice for the filling so that it retains some bite can make these especially toothsome. Being generous with the dried shiitake and shrimps and peanuts helps a great deal, too.

A png kueh mould is required for this. They come in either plastic or wood, etched with an array of different patterns. They can vary in size, but only slightly, seldom affecting the yield.

If the idea of food dye rankles, please consider using beetroot juice or sieved pink dragonfruit pulp.

MAKES 8

for the filling
175g glutinous rice
30g raw peanuts, unskinned
6 dried shiitake mushrooms
40g dried shrimp
3 tbsp vegetable oil, plus more for
    brushing
2 shallots, peeled and chopped
2 garlic, peeled and finely chopped
¼ tsp salt
1 tsp light soy sauce
1 tsp fish sauce
Pinch of caster sugar
Pinch of finely ground white pepper

for the pastry
175g rice flour
50g tapioca starch
¼ tsp salt
350ml boiling water
A few drops pink food colouring
Eight 15cm banana leaf squares,
    cleaned

to serve
Sweet flour sauce

Wash the glutinous rice three times or until the water runs clear. Place in a bowl and soak in a generous amount of water for at least 6 hours or overnight.

Soak the raw peanuts in a bowl of water for 1 hour or until they swell and soften slightly. Steep the dried shiitake mushrooms in 200ml boiling water for 30 minutes or until supple. Rinse the dried shrimp and soak in a small bowl of cold water for 10 minutes.

Drain the peanuts and dried shrimp and contain them in separate bowls. Drain the shiitake, reserving 4 tbsp of the soaking liquor. Cut off their stalks and finely dice their caps.

Prepare a steamer, filling its lower compartment with plenty of water and lining its perforated tray with muslin cloth. Drain the glutinous rice, spread it out over the muslin-tined tray, then steam over high heat for 30 minutes. Sprinkle with 3 tbsp water, stir briefly, and steam for another 15 minutes or until tender but with a hint of bite. Leave to cool slightly. Do not wash the steamer just yet.

Now make the pastry: place the rice flour, tapioca starch and salt in a bowl and stir in the boiling water and pink food dye until clumps begin to form. Cover and leave for 15 minutes, then go in with your paws and massage until well incorporated and smooth. Cover and leave for 30 minutes while you complete the filling.

Heat the vegetable oil in a deep frying pan or wide saucepan over medium heat. Once hot, add the shallots and fry until fragrant and translucent. Then add the garlic, fry until fragrant, then stir in the dried shrimp. Fry for 2 minutes, then add the chopped shiitake and peanuts and fry for another 2 minutes.

Add the cooked glutinous rice, the reserved 4 tbsp mushroom soaking liquor, salt, light soy, fish sauce, caster sugar and white pepper. Fry for 2-3 minutes, stirring well, then taste and adjust seasoning with salt. Cover and leave to cool until just warm to touch.

Divide the rested pastry into 8 portions, then roll each into a ball. Flatten a ball in your palm, pile 2-3 tbsp of the filling on its middle, bring up the sides to conceal and roll it back into a ball. Lightly flour both the *png kueh* and its mould, then press the former into the latter with your palm. Sharply tap the mould against the counter, thereby freeing the *kueh*. Make them all this way.

Lightly oil the banana leaf squares and arrange the *kueh* on them. Trim these leaf squares to match their cargos' silhouettes, leaving a 1cm track around them.

Top up the water in your steamer if need be and put it over medium heat. Arrange the *kueh* in the perforated steamer tray. Place this on the steamer, cover, reduce the heat to medium-low and steam for 20 minutes. (Too fierce a heat may result in the pastries swelling drastically, dissolving their patterned faces.) Remove from the heat, cool for 2-3 minutes, then brush with vegetable oil to prevent them from drying out.

You may eat these as they are, with a slick of sweet flour sauce, but I prefer them pan-fried and eaten with daubs of garlicky chilli sauce (always from a bottle).

FRIED SQUID WITH SAMBAL & PLUM SAUCE

This was something we used to eat during the occasional meal at the home of our paternal grandmother, bought in from a nearby chicken rice shop. There is evidently nothing Teochew about it, though one could nub out the plum sauce in the spirit of generosity.

The stipulated frying time for the squid may seem an error but is not. The sound of them clattering against the sides of the pan should be enough to intimidate teeth back into gums. They soften slightly once slicked in sauce, eating like sweet, spicy, sticky cephalapod popcorn. Intense and addictive. Have some Trachisan ready.

SERVES 4

250g medium squid, cleaned
60g cornflour
40g potato starch
Two pinches of salt
Water, approx. 3-4 tbsp
2½ tbsp plum sauce
1 tbsp *sambal belacan* (page 219)
Peanut oil, for deep-frying

to serve
Calamansi limes

Thinly slice the prepared squid and place in a bowl. Sprinkle over the cornflour, potato starch and salt and mix well. Add enough water to form a velvety slurry thick enough to coat the squid.

Heat 4cm of peanut oil in a wide, deep frying pan over medium heat. Once hot but not smoking, add the squid, first shaking off excess batter. Their first instinct is to clump, so gently disperse them with a pair of tongs, then fry for 12-15 minutes, until crisp and golden. Remove the fried squid to a plate lined with kitchen towel and leave to cool slightly.

In a medium-sized mixing bowl, combine the plum sauce and *sambal belacan*. Shoot in the fried squid and mix. It will be a snug fit: the squid should be radiant and gleaming, not dripping and hungover. Add a touch more plum sauce and *sambal* if the squid looks parched.

Plate up and serve with calamansi limes for very necessary acid.

HEI ZHO 虾枣

This is similar to ngo hiong, the main difference being that it is cut into sections after steaming, dusted in cornflour and deep-fried. Some restaurants forego the beancurd skins entirely, dropping spoonfuls of the prawn-pork filling into gurgling oil and serving the ragged-edged balls with bowls of plum sauce or vinegary chilli sauce.

Do not use lean pork; some fat is necessary. It should also be coarsely minced, as this will make for a more satisfying texture.

Take extra care when wiping the beancurd sheets. You have to be thorough as they are fiendishly salty, but also gentle as they are extremely fragile. In moments like this, life can truly seem impossible.

SERVES 6-8

500g prawn flesh
125g pork belly, skinned weight
2 garlic cloves, peeled and minced
2 small red onions, peeled and finely
   chopped
2 spring onions, finely sliced
50g carrot, minced
125g water chestnuts, peeled weight,
   cut into fine dice
2 tbsp chopped coriander leaves
¼ tsp ground white pepper
1½ tsp light soy sauce
1 tsp fish sauce
¾ tsp salt
Pinch of caster sugar
1 tsp five spice powder
1 medium egg, lighten beaten
1½ tbsp cornflour, plus more to
   coat
10 dried beancurd sheets, approx.
   20x25cm
Vegetable oil, for deep-frying

to serve
Sweet flour sauce or plum sauce

With a cleaver, chop the prawns into small pieces, then roughly mince them. Place in a bowl. Do the same with the pork belly and add it to the prawns. Add the garlic, red onions, spring onions, carrot, water chestnuts, coriander, white pepper, light soy sauce, fish sauce, salt, caster sugar, five spice powder, beaten egg and cornflour. Stir to combine thoroughly, but gently, as overmixing will lead to toughness. Cover and refrigerate for an hour or so.

Prepare your steamer, filling its lower compartment with plenty of water and placing it over medium-high heat.

Gingerly wipe the beancurd sheets numerous times with wet kitchen towel to remove excess salt. Divide the prawn-pork mixture among these sheets, smear their edges with water and roll them into tight logs. Lightly prong them with a toothpick and arrange them on a wide heatproof dish. Lower this into the steamer and steam for 10-12 minutes, until springy and cooked. Remove from the steamer and allow to cool.

Heat 4cm of vegetable oil in a wide saucepan or wok over medium heat. Cut the *hei zho* into 2cm sections and roll them in a shallow dish of cornflour until lightly coated. Deep-fry the *hei zho* in batches to a rich golden turn. The oil will become disconcertingly cloudy in the process but worry not: this is normal.

Serve with your choice of sauce.

ZHU JIAO DONG 猪脚冻

I have memories of visiting the food centre at Jalan Berseh with my father on weekends. He would order this, lucent tiles of pork trotter jelly; a plate of steamed shark and its liver, an attendant saucer bearing an ointment of chilli and crushed peanuts; a limpid broth with cloud fungus and jujubes; and a couple of bowls of hot rice. We would then walk over to the food court along Kelantan Lane and have laksa. This was his idea of a light lunch.

It has now become common to replace the pig's skin required to set the jelly with gelatine, in a bid to make it more crystalline in clarity and, perhaps, less intensely porky. I see character in some murkiness and so much rather do it the trad way.

If your trotter still has some hair, turn it over a lit burner to singe them off.

SERVES 8-10

1kg pig trotter, cleaned (see above)
2 litres water
2 garlic cloves
5cm ginger, crushed
1 tsp white peppercorns
15g rock sugar
1 tsp fish sauce
1 tsp light soy sauce
1 tsp dark soy sauce
1 tsp salt
500g pig's skin

for the chilli sauce
2 garlic cloves, peeled
5 red chillies, sliced
1 bird's eye chilli, sliced
150ml water
1 tbsp rice vinegar
½ tsp fish sauce
½ tsp caster sugar
¼ tsp salt, plus more to taste

to serve
Chinese celery leaves, roughly chopped

Bring a large pot of water to a boil over high heat, then add the trotter. Blanch for 5 minutes, then drain and wash under a running tap. Briefly rinse the pot, return the trotter to it, then cover with the 2 litres water. Add the garlic, ginger, white peppercorns, rock sugar, fish sauce, light and dark soy sauces and salt. Bring to a boil over high heat, cover, reduce the heat and simmer for 1 hour.

Uncover the pot, add the skin, reinstate the cover and simmer for another hour. Then, uncover again, remove both trotter and skin to a plate and leave to cool. Meanwhile, raise the heat and reduce the pork stock to 950ml.

Slice half the skin into thin strips. (Reserve the other half, drying them in a low oven into chips and frying it into *chicharon*.) Cut the trotter meat into chunks. Arrange the chunked trotter and sliced skin in a 16 x 22 x 5cm tin and pour over the stock. Give the tin a shake, cover and refrigerate overnight.

For the sauce, blend the ingredients until smooth, tip into a small saucepan and simmer over medium-low heat for just 5 minutes, so it thickens slightly and loses some of its rawness. Cool completely and adjust seasoning with salt.

Remove the jelly from the cold 30 minutes before eating time. Invert onto a chopping board, slice as you desire and arrange on a platter. Sprinkle with the Chinese celery leaves and serve with the chilli sauce.

PORK BELLY WITH SOY, GARLIC & CHILLI 咸肚肉

Its name in Chinese means "salted pork belly", which is but a fraction of the story. After being salted, the meat is boiled, cooled, carved and eaten alongside a sauce of chilli, garlic and soy. It is one of those Teochew dishes mostly encountered in homes. I have been told, however, that some cai png vendors have it snuck in amongst their plethora of offerings.

Do not be startled by the seemingly meagre quantity of meat: it goes further than you would think.

SERVES 4-6

350g piece of pork belly
2½ tsp salt
1 litre water
1 garlic clove, bruised
2cm ginger, bruised

for the sauce
2 garlic cloves, finely chopped
3 bird's eye chillies, finely sliced
3 tbsp light soy sauce
2 tbsp water

to serve
Leaves from a bunch of coriander sprigs
Calamansi limes, halved

Massage the pork belly thoroughly with the salt, then place on a tray and refrigerate it for 6-8 hours.

Give the belly a good rinse to remove excess salt, then place it in a medium-sized saucepan with the water, garlic clove and ginger. Bring to a boil over high heat, then cover, reduce the heat and simmer gently for 45-50 minutes or until the meat is tender. An inserted skewer should slide in with ease. Remove and leave to cool completely. (You may elect to refrigerate it overnight.) Reserve the stock for future use, in a soup or braise.

Carve the meat into thin slices, arrange on a platter and strew with the coriander leaves and halved calamansi limes. Serve with the sauce, which you make quite simply by whirling everything together.

TEOCHEW STEAMED POMFRET 潮州式蒸白鯧

Other than the kind of fish here, which has to be silver or white pomfret, freshness is paramount. The seasonings are gentle, so there is no masking any ill qualities.

Common as it is to steam the fish in a shallow pool of plain water, I do what some cooks do and add a little fish sauce. Others replace the water with chicken or clean-tasting fish stock instead for that extra soupçon of savouriness.

For this you require salted mustard greens, not their sour preserved counterparts. Both tend to be sold in hermetically sealed pouches in liquid tinted to varying degrees of yellow, so be sure to read the labels carefully.

The sort of sour plums to use here are the ones sold in bottles of brine.

It is traditional to arrange thin slices of boiled pork fat across the fish just before it goes into the steamer, but this is not something we do much in our house. Nor do we bother with squares of silken tofu. The choice is yours.

SERVES 4

125g salted mustard greens (*kiam chai*)
400-450g white pomfret, cleaned
40g ginger, peeled and thinly sliced
2 sprigs coriander, roots intact
3 red bird's eye chillies, slit
4 dried shiitake mushrooms,
   soaked and thinly sliced (page 219)
5 sour plums, lightly crushed
2 medium tomatoes, quartered
100ml water (see above)
2 tsp fish sauce
2 spring onions, cut into 4cm segments

Prepare your steamer.

Rinse the salted mustard greens and soak in a bowl of water for 15 minutes to remove surfeit salt. Drain well and thinly slice.

Score the cleaned pomfret 2-3 times on either side. Feed a third of the ginger into its belly cavity. Slice the roots off the coriander sprigs, lightly bruise them, and feed these in as well. Reserve the leafy portion of the sprigs.

Arrange another third of the sliced ginger on the base of a wide heatproof dish and rest the fish on top. Strew over the remaining ginger, red bird's eye chillies, sliced shiitake mushrooms, sour plums, tomatoes and salted mustard greens. Pour over the water and sprinkle over the fish sauce. Steam for 6-8 minutes.

Remove from the steamer. Strew over the spring onions and coriander leafage and serve at once with rice.

YU PIAN MI FEN 鱼片米粉

A clean-tasting, white-fleshed fish, like grouper, red snapper or barramundi, is ideal here. While flesh and bones need not come from the same kind of fish, it is preferable that they at least come from similar tasting ones.

For the stock, the bones are fried and simmered in liquid (along with chicken feet) for several hours, which chefs may raise an eyebrow at, given the gluey taste that can arise from boiling fish for too long. So far I have had no huge issues with this.

For a fuller, milkier broth, strain the stock through a sieve and reserve the fish bones. Blend the bones in a liquidiser with the stock and strain once more, this time through a sieve with especially fine mesh.

SERVES 4

for the broth
1¼kg fish bones (see above)
600g chicken feet, trimmed
3 garlic cloves, peeled
175g ginger, peeled and crushed
6 spring onions, white portion only
2½ litres water
2 tsp light soy sauce
2 tsp fish sauce
4 tbsp Shaoxing rice wine
2 tsp white peppercorns, toasted
2 tsp salt
Peanut oil, for frying

for the fish
350g white fish fillet (see above), thinly
    sliced
2 tsp cornflour
2 tsp light soy sauce
2 tsp fish sauce

to finish
400g fresh thick rice vermicelli
200g Beijing cabbage, roughly chunked
2 tomato, quartered
4 spring onions, cut into 4cm sections
2 tbsp Shaoxing rice wine
Salt, finely ground white pepper

to serve
Light soy sauce
Red bird's eye chillies, finely sliced

Heat 3cm peanut oil in a deep frying pan or wok over medium-high heat. Once hot, fry the fish bones until golden. Drain off the oil and add the fried bones to a large saucepan. Add the chicken feet, garlic, ginger, spring onions, water, light soy sauce, fish sauce, Shaoxing rice wine, white peppercorns and salt. Bring to a boil over high heat, then cover, reduce the heat and simmer for 2½ hours, or until the broth is flavourful and slightly cloudy.

Strain the stock into a fresh pot through a fine mesh sieve, pressing to extract as much goodness as possible. Set aside.

Combine the sliced fish with the cornflour, light soy sauce and fish sauce. Set aside for 30 minutes.

Place the thick rice vermicelli in a colander and rinse under a warm tap.

Bring the broth to a boil, then add the marinated fish slices and cabbage. Once the fish turns opaque, add the rice noodles, tomatoes, spring onions and Shaoxing rice wine. Simmer for 2 minutes, then taste and adjust seasoning with salt and finely ground white pepper.

Divide among 4 waiting bowls and serve with little dishes of light soy sauce and sliced red bird's eye chillies.

LOR ARK 卤鸭

I used to watch our domestics braise duck under the supervision of my mother in our wet kitchen, basting and turning the bird in the calloused, cast iron wok of bubbling, chocolate-deep sauce until it was dark and glossy as a conker.

The use of pandan leaf is not traditional, but it seems to add a mellowness and behaves as a kind of mediator for the array of voices at work.

SERVES 6

for the duck
1 x 2kg duck, without head and feet
2 tbsp dark soy sauce
1 tbsp Shaoxing rice wine

to cook
60g yellow rock sugar, crushed
12 garlic cloves, peeled and crushed
4 shallots, peeled
100g galangal, peeled and bruised
50g old ginger, peeled and bruised
3 tbsp Shaoxing rice wine
125ml dark soy sauce
75ml light soy sauce
4 cinnamon sticks
5 cloves
4 star anise
2 tsp white peppercorns
2 spring onions
1 pandan blade, knotted
¼ tsp salt, plus more to taste
2 tsp dark brown sugar
6 boiled eggs, peeled
   (page 219)
Water

to serve
2 small cucumbers, halved and
   thinly sliced on a diagonal
Small bunch of coriander sprigs

Massage the cleaned duck, inside and out, with the dark soy sauce and Shaoxing rice wine. Cover and refrigerate for at least 2 hours or overnight.

Remove the duck from the cold an hour before cooking. The dark soy sauce and rice wine should have been mostly absorbed by the duck. Sear the duck in a large wok over high heat, for about 1 minute per side. Remove it to a platter.

To the wok, add the yellow rock sugar. Allow the sugar to melt and caramelise until light amber. Add 3 tbsp water, let it sizzle and splutter, then add the garlic, shallots, galangal and old ginger. Stir for 30 seconds, then add the 3 tbsp Shaoxing rice wine, dark and light soy sauces, cinnamon sticks, cloves, star anise, white peppercorns, spring onions, pandan blade, salt and dark brown sugar. Allow this dark, spicy liquid to come a rolling boil, then gently lower in the duck. Pour enough water to cover it by two-thirds. Once the liquid simmers robustly, turn the heat down to its lowest setting, cover and simmer for 1½ hours, turning the bird over every 15 minutes. Add the peeled eggs during the last 20 minutes of this simmering period.

When the duck has had its 1½ hours, remove it, together with the eggs, to a platter to cool. Raise the heat beneath the wok and boil the liquid until it has reduced by half, about 15 minutes.

Carve the cooled duck with a cleaver and arrange on a serving platter. Halve the eggs and arrange them around the bird and nap with the rich sauce. Finish with cucumber slices and coriander.

BRAISED BITTERGOURD WITH PORK RIBS

苦瓜炒咸菜焖排骨

This recipe was kindly supplied by my aunt. It succumbed to minor tinkering: I added ginger and made sure there was a tiny bit more sauce to lubricate those non-negotiable bowls of rice.

The bittergourd used here is the mild-tasting, pale-green sort, with gentle bumps and grooves as opposed to spikes.

The fermented black beans (or more accurately, black soy beans) used here are not those sold in bottles of inky brine, but dry, slightly wrinkled and sandy with salt.

SERVES 6-8

300g salted mustard greens (*kiam chai*)
1½ tbsp fermented black beans
2 tbsp vegetable oil
4 garlic cloves, peeled and chopped
5cm ginger, peeled and slivered
500g pork ribs, cut into 5cm pieces
2 tomatoes, cut into quarters
Salt, to taste
350ml water or chicken stock (page 221)
1 large Chinese bittergourd, approx.
    500g

Rinse the salted mustard greens and soak in a bowl of water for 15 minutes to remove surfeit salt. Drain and cut into thick pieces and set aside.

Briefly rinse the fermented black beans, then soak in a bowl of water for 15 minutes. Drain and set aside.

Heat the vegetable oil in a large saucepan over medium heat. Once hot, add the garlic and ginger, and fry until fragrant and lightly coloured. Add the fermented black beans and fry for a minute. Add the pork ribs, stirring to seal, then the tomatoes, a pinch of salt and the salted mustard greens. Pour over the water or stock, bring to a boil, then cover, reduce the heat and simmer gently for 1 hour.

Meanwhile, halve and deseed the bittergourd, then cut these halves into 4cm sections. Add these to the pot, cover and simmer for another 45 minutes, stirring occasionally and gently, until very soft. I quite like it as is, but if you prefer it drier, remove the lid 15 minutes before the end of the cooking time. Most of the liquid will cook off, leaving you with just a bit of gloss. Eat with plenty of rice.

HU JIAO ZHU DU TANG 胡椒猪肚汤

Despite this soup of pig's stomach and pepper being an incredibly basic Teochew dish, I did not get into it until my university days, having been put off offal in general by encounters with sandy, ferrous slices of overcooked pig liver. Had this been my starting point, the outcome would have been different, as pig's stomach is not so much about taste but texture, fleshiness with a touch of resistance.

In the Philippines, I was taught to wash pig's stomach and intestines with flour and vinegar or lime juice, and have not stopped since. It is a surprisingly calming activity. If only doing the laundry gave me as much satisfaction.

You may replace a portion of the white peppercorns with their black counterpart and perhaps reduce the amount slightly if it seems excessive. I happen to like a broth so hot that it cools.

SERVES 4

2½ tbsp white peppercorns
500g pork ribs, cut into 4cm pieces
1½ litres water
6 garlic cloves, skins on
¼ tsp caster sugar
1 tsp salt, plus more to taste
500g whole pig's stomach
Approx. 4-6 tbsp rice vinegar
Approx. 4-6 tbsp plain flour

Warm the white peppercorns in a small frying pan, then crush them with a pestle and mortar into a coarse powder.

Half-fill a large saucepan with water and bring it to a boil over high heat. Add the pork ribs and blanch for 5 minutes, then drain and rinse under a running tap. Return the ribs to the saucepan, add the 1½ litres water, garlic, caster sugar, salt and the crushed peppercorns. Bring to a boil over high heat, then reduce the heat and simmer gently for 45 minutes.

Meanwhile, clean the pig's stomach: massage it with loving thoroughness, inside and out, with 1-2 tbsp of the vinegar and the same of flour. Wash it thoroughly and repeat once or twice, until it smells pleasing (or least displeasing). Set aside.

When the broth has had its 45 minutes, add the cleaned pig's stomach whole and simmer for 45 minutes, until just tender.

Tong out the stomach and slice it into 1½cm slices. Return it to the pot and cook for another 30 minutes. By now, the ribs and stomach pieces should be very tender. Taste and adjust seasoning with salt.

SUGARED TARO 反沙芋

This recipe, and the orh nee some pages down, is a staple dessert at most Teochew restaurants. There is something about the conjunction between sugary crust and powdery interior, that makes for quite a gratifying experience.

SERVES 6

450g taro yam, peeled and cut
    into 1½cm sticks
150g caster sugar
2 tbsp water
Peanut oil, for deep-frying

Heat 4cm of peanut oil in a deep saucepan (or wok) over medium heat. Once hot but not smoking, add the prepared taro. Fry for 3-4 minutes, until just cooked through and barely coloured. Drain them on kitchen towel.

Decant the oil into a large bowl, discarding it once it has cooled. Wash the saucepan thoroughly, dry it and add the caster sugar and water. Place the pan over medium heat and stir until the sugar has melted. Reduce the heat slightly and let the syrup continue cooking until it reaches thread stage. (If it helps, it should possess the viscosity and heaviness of thick honey.) Turn off the heat. Add the fried taro and turn them over in the syrup that will inevitably crystallise around them. Serve at once.

SWEET LONGEVITY NOODLES 长寿面

My paternal grandmother used to make this for her children on their birthdays, a nest of wheat noodles, roughly the thickness of ramen, in a pond of sugar syrup, boosted with a pair of hardboiled eggs. It is, to be entirely honest, an acquired taste. This recipe includes pandan, ginger and goji berries, which add personality by way of fragrance and flavour.

The noodles in question are, in fact, commonly sold as longevity noodles. Rough, rigid, with a faintly plastic appeal, some may find them more suited to the stationary drawer than the larder. The shades in which they come, a muted white and lurid orange, do little to alter this opinion. But it is this toughness they possess, a modicum of which is retained after boiling, that enables them to stand up to the sugary liquid.

SERVES 2

100g rock sugar, crushed
20g ginger, thinly sliced
1 pandan blade, knotted
1 tsp goji berries
1 litre water
150g longevity noodles
4 hardboiled eggs, peeled

Place the rock sugar, ginger, pandan blade, goji berries and water in a medium saucepan. Bring to a boil over medium heat, then lower the heat and simmer for 5 minutes, stirring until the sugar dissolves.

Cook the longevity noodles based on the packet's instructions. Drain in a colander and rinse under cold water to remove excess starch.

Divide the noodles between 2 bowls and ladle over the hot syrup. Tuck 2 hardboiled eggs into each bowl and serve.

TAU SUAN 豆爽

It does seem odd that a mess of cooked dal, suspended in viscous syrup, with sections of snipped-up fried dough, could ever provide the pleasure it does. The split moong dal afford more than powdery bite, but a sandy earthiness that foils the sweet, pandan-scented liquid.

The addition of coconut sugar (gula melaka), a mere tablespoon's worth, is not traditional but works, weaving in notes of caramel along with sweetness.

SERVES 4

100g split and peeled mung beans (*moong dal*)
60g rock sugar
15g coconut sugar (*gula melaka*), shaved
650ml water, plus 2 tbsp
2 pandan blades
5 tsp potato starch
Pinch of salt

to serve
You tiao (page 33)

Pick over the *moong dal*, removing any impurities, then wash in a sieve under a running tap. Tip into a bowl, cover with water and soak for at least 6 hours or overnight.

The following day, prepare your steamer, filling its lower compartment with plenty of water. Place over high heat and bring to a boil. Line the perforated steamer tray with muslin cloth.

Drain the *moong dal* and spread them over the lined steamer tray. Once the steamer is boiling, pop the tray on, cover and cook for 12-15 minutes, or until the *dal* is cooked but not mushy; each grain should remain distinct and separate. Remove the cooked *dal* to a bowl and set aside.

In a medium saucepan, combine the rock sugar, *gula melaka*, 650ml water and pandan blades. Bring to a boil over high heat, then lower the flame and simmer for 2-3 minutes, stirring until the sugars have dissolved. Tip in the cooked *moong dal* and simmer for another 2-3 minutes, just so both pulse and liquid can get aquainted.

In a small bowl, mix the 2 tbsp water with the potato starch, then pour this slurry into the saucepan, stirring. The liquid will thicken almost immediately, but grant it another 3-4 minutes to bubble anyway. This promises an even consistency. Taste and adjust seasoning with salt.

Tong out the pandan blades and distribute among 4 waiting bowls. Snip over the *you tiao* (page 33) and serve.

ORH NEE 芋泥

Orh nee, at its most stripped back, involves frying crushed taro yam in lard with a little sugar. The scent and flavour of the lard really permeates the grey mash, its texture so dense and thick that you could stand a spoon in it. The recipe provided here is aligned with modern renditions, a fragrant syrup of pandan and rock sugar cajoled into its body.

SERVES 6

500g taro yam, peeled weight, cut into
  2cm chunks
150g yellow rock sugar, crushed
1 pandan blade
300ml water
8 tbsp vegetable oil
3 shallots, peeled and finely sliced
1 tbsp lard

Fill a steamer with plenty of water and place over high heat. Put the taro chunks in its perforated compartment and steam for 20-25 minutes or until tender.

Meanwhile, make a syrup by combining the yellow rock sugar, pandan blade and water in a small saucepan. Bring to a boil over medium-high heat, then reduce the heat and simmer for 5-7 minutes or until the sugar has melted and the pandan blade looks wizened and spent. Set aside.

When the taro is cooked, tip them out into a bowl and mash thoroughly with a spatula or a potato masher.

Heat the vegetable oil in a wok or deep frying pan over medium-low heat. Add the shallots and cook for 7-10 mins until they are crisp and have infused the oil with their sweetness. Remove the shallots with a slotted spoon (you may save them for something else) and add the crushed taro. Continue cooking over medium-low heat for 12-15 minutes, stirring constantly, until it has acquired a reddish tinge and is fragrant.

Strain in the pandan syrup and continue cooking for another 15 minutes, stirring gently, until the *orh ni* is thick and glossy. Stir in the lard. Once this is absorbed, the dish is done.

note
This is commonly served with sweetened gingko nuts. Halve and remove the pits from 50g peeled raw gingko nuts, then simmer them in a light syrup made with 40g rock sugar, 225ml water and a knotted blade of pandan until waxily tender and lucent, about 15-20 minutes.

How I slipped into baking as a child remains a bit of a mystery to me. We seldom had cakes, tarts or buns occupying counter or fridge space at home. Apart from sliced bread, Danish butter cookies, synonymous with their eye-catching blue tins, was the only baked treat we made sure to stock, mostly because my grandmother loved them. Toothsome, perhaps, but not incredibly stirring.

Nevertheless, I began with cake mixes and gradually worked my way up to, and then through, the cookbooks cluttering our cabinets. It was a battered copy of *The Margaret Fulton Cookbook* that had me especially enraptured with its jam rolls, rock buns and butter and orange cakes. This inclination towards confections that many these days would deem prosaic was not just due to greenness but a preference of crumb over cream. Indeed, no one at home cared much for icings or high-octane embellishments at the time.

Now that baking puts bread on my family's table, I find myself missing the levity, silliness, even uncertainty, suffusing those early years. On the occasion that a cake I bring into this world appears a little wonky, any disappointment is quickly displaced by a sense of fatalistic cheer.

All creative activities are collaborations. This applies to one-man shows too, and those of the kitchen are no exception, with working partnerships lying between the agent, ingredients, equipment and environment. But while cooking often permits intervention, baking is less permissive, only granting involvement at the beginning and at the end. Even the most qualified professional cannot claim to possess utter control of the process every single time, much less the result. There is beauty in that.

BUTTER CAKE

The cake that will greet you at the end of these instructions is moist and rich enough to be contemplated in thin slices with coffee or brandy, not one of those airy creatures you'd find floating on the coffee shop counters of yesteryear.

This recipe involves a 2½-litre bundt tin but also works a joy in a 24-26cm ring tin of similar capacity.

SERVES 12

350g plain flour
1¼ tsp baking powder
½ tsp baking soda
125ml milk
150ml whipping cream
2 tsp vinegar
250g unsalted butter, softened
375g caster sugar
1 tsp salt
4 extra large eggs
   (250g without shell)
1½ tsp vanilla extract
1½ tbsp brandy
Vegetable oil, for lubricating tin

for the icing
200g icing sugar, sieved
1-2 tbsp milk

Preheat the oven to 170°C. Lubricate a fluted 2½-litre bundt tin with vegetable oil.

Combine the plain flour, baking powder and soda in a large bowl.

Combine the milk, whipping cream and vinegar in a measuring jug. Leave to stand for 10 minutes.

Cream the softened butter with the caster sugar and salt in a free-standing electric mixer fitted with a whisk attachment until very pale and airy. Introduce the eggs one at a time, only adding the next when the previous has been incorporated. (If the batter seems on the cusp of splitting, add a spoonful of the flour mixture.) Continue beating until the batter is moussey and thick, about a minute or so.

Add half the leavened flour and half the soured milk and let the machine incorporate these into the batter at a medium speed. Do the same for the remaining portions of both, vanilla extract and brandy. The resultant batter should be smooth, creamy and thick, but not stiff.

Transfer the batter to the prepared tin and smooth its surface. Give it several light raps against the kitchen counter, then bake on a centre shelf for 45-50 minutes until gold and a skewer inserted into its thickest part emerges clean.

Leave the cake to compose itself for 10 minutes. Say a little prayer, upend it onto a wire rack and let it cool completely.

Make the icing, very simply, by mixing the sieved icing sugar with enough milk to get a thick, pourable paint. Dribble this over the cooled cake and let it set crisply before taking a blade to its body.

SUGEE CAKE

A Eurasian staple for birthdays and special occasions, this is not a lightweight concoction, its body bold and sandy with almonds and semolina, its namesake. Most recipes call for a perfume of vanilla and almond extracts. This version also benefits from the addition of brandy and rose water. Orange blossom water, though untraditional, is also magic in this.

Another quality associated with sugee cake must surely be extravagance. Much to the anxiety of novice bakers and dieticians, a recipe for a single wheel can demand a dozen egg yolks and a pound of butter. The former group may find comfort in the modest loaf this recipe produces; there is no need to wait for an event to make a commitment. As for the latter, I cannot reduce the horror but prevent its swelling: this particular cake is left plain, spared the marzipan and futon of royal icing it so often receives.

SERVES 8

125g semolina
200g unsalted butter, softened
60g blanched almonds
55g plain flour
½ tsp baking powder
4 egg yolks, plus 1 white
175g caster sugar
½ tsp salt
85ml evaporated milk
2 tsp vanilla extract
2 tsp rose water
1½ tsp brandy
¼ tsp almond extract, *optional*

Combine the semolina and 75g of the unsalted butter in a bowl amd mix well. Cover and leave in a cool place for at least 8 hours or overnight.

Preheat the oven to 175°C. Spread the blanched almonds out on a baking sheet and toast them for 7-9 minutes, or until fragrant but lightly coloured. Remove from the oven and allow to cool completely.

Reduce the oven temperature to 150°C. Line a 21 x 10cm loaf tin with greaseproof paper.

Blend the cool, toasted almonds with the plain flour into a mostly fine rubble; a hint of coarseness is ideal. Tip into a large bowl, then mix in the butter-soaked semolina and baking powder until well combined.

Whisk the egg yolks, caster sugar and salt in a freestanding electric mixer until thick, mousse-like and pale. Add the remaining 125g unsalted butter and whisk until creamily incorporated.

Fold in the almond-semolina rubble in two parts, until well combined. Add the evaporated milk, vanilla extract, rose water, brandy and almond extract, if using, and fold in thoroughly.

Whisk the single egg white in a small bowl until it reaches stiff peak stage. Fold this into the cake batter, then scrape the lot into the prepared loaf tin.

Give the tin several raps on the cake counter to expel any air pockets, then bake on the centre shelf for 45-55 minutes. The cooked loaf should be golden and evenly risen, though a teensy bit tender in the middle. An inserted skewer should emerge shiny with grease but devoid of raw batter.

Leave the cake to cool in its tin for 30 minutes. Transfer it to a wire rack, strip off the protective paper and cool completely before slicing and serving.

CHOCOLATE CAKE

The cake this recipe makes is not double or trible layered. It is not perfumed with spice nor lubricated with alcohol. Nor does it receive any outladish flourishes. It is an elegant creature, slim and dark in its coat of ganache.

SERVES 8

for the cake
65ml cream
65ml milk
1 tsp cider vinegar
125ml vegetable oil
1 tsp vanilla extract
150g plain flour
25g cocoa powder
175g caster sugar
1 tsp baking powder
½ tsp baking soda
¼ tsp salt
1 egg
1 egg yolk
125ml boiling water

for the ganache
200g dark chocolate, finely chopped
Pinch of salt
75g unsalted butter
75g condensed milk
75ml whipping cream
1 tsp vanilla extract

Preheat the oven to 160°C. Line the base and sides of a 20 x 5cm round cake tin with greaseproof paper.

Combine the cream, milk and cider vinegar in a measuring jug and leave to stand for 10 minutes. Once the dairy has thickened, whisk in the vegetable oil and vanilla extract.

Place the plain flour, cocoa powder, caster sugar, baking powder and soda and salt in a free-standing electric mixer fitted with a whisk attachment. Let the machine whir at medium speed, to combine the ingredients.

Beat in the egg and the yolk at medium speed. When they seem unable to absorb anymore of the dry stuff, add the emulsion of milk, cream and oil. Raise the speed to medium-high and beat for 1 minute or until the batter lightens by a shade and its surface is thinly covered in bubbles. Pour in the boiling water with the motor running and once this has been absorbed, turn off the machine. Pour the liquid batter into the prepared tin and bake on a centre shelf for 35-45 minutes or until springy. A skewer inserted into the thickest part should emerge clean, too. Allow the cake to cool in its tin.

Make the ganache. Place the dark chocolate and salt in a bowl. Heat the butter and condensed milk in a small saucepan until hand-hot, then pour over the chocolate. Leave for a minute, stir until smooth, then whisk in the cream and vanilla extract.

Free the cake from its tin, discarding the protective paper, and place it on a serving platter. Frost the cake with ganache as you desire, with a palette knife. Tidy the serving platter with kitchen towel and let the ganache set slightly for about 1 hour before serving. Or not.

COFFEE CAKES

These are sweet-looking and straightforward, in both method and overall effect.

I use 75ml dariole moulds, usually made of aluminium, but you may use paper muffin cups of similar stature instead.

The icing, decidedly old-fashioned, is sweet, but also thin, crisp and faintly bitter, sending off the sugariness before it can even think about lingering.

For the accompanying photograph, I could not find chocolate-coated coffee beans with which to decorate and so, for amusement, used chocolates shaped like coffee beans.

MAKES 15

2½ tbsp instant coffee powder
2 tbsp boiling water
110ml milk
100ml cream
2 tsp vinegar
190g plain flour
2 tsp baking powder
¼ tsp baking soda
125g unsalted butter, softened
190g caster sugar
Pinch of salt
2 eggs

for the icing
2½ tsp instant coffee powder
1 tbsp boiling water
300g icing sugar
2 tbsp cream
Approx. 2-3 tsp water

to finish
15 chocolate-coated coffee beans

Preheat the oven to 175°C. Lightly grease 15 x 75ml dariole moulds.

In a jug, dissolve the instant coffee powder in the boiling water. Stir in the milk, cream and vinegar. Set aside.

Combine the plain flour, baking powder and soda in a bowl.

In a freestanding mixer fitted with a paddle attachment, beat the butter, caster sugar and salt at medium speed until pale and creamy, about a minute. Beat in the eggs, one at a time, until slightly aerated, about 30 seconds. Add the leavened flour and let the machine mix it in at medium speed. Stream in the coffee-flavoured milk and once the batter is smooth (and quite runny), it is done.

Divide the batter among the 15 greased moulds. Bake at a centre shelf for 20 minutes or until springy. Remove from the oven and let them relax in their moulds for 5 minutes. Then unmould and arrange them on a wire rack to cool completely.

Once the cakes are cool, make the icing. Dissolve the instant coffee powder into the boiling water, then add it with the cream to the icing sugar. Stir to mix, adding just enough water to yield a thick paint, then dollop over the small cakes. Press a chocolate-coated coffee bean on each darling, then abandon for an hour, or until the icing crisply sets.

GOLDEN SYRUP CAKE

Although this exact cake did not figure in my youth, it reminds me a great deal of the ginger bread and treacle tart that did, having first read about them in novels.

A word of caution: the Horlicks cream is meant to be softly set, so I would not recommend leaving this cake out on a warm day for too long.

SERVES 8

100ml milk
1 tsp cider vinegar
1 tsp vanilla extract
2 eggs
150g unsalted butter
2 tbsp vegetable oil
250g golden syrup
50g caster sugar
Pinch of salt
225g plain flour
½ tsp baking powder
1 tsp baking soda

for the frosting
75g cool unsalted butter, cubed
350g cold cream cheese, cubed
90g icing sugar
75g condensed milk
1 tsp vanilla extract
3 tbsp Horlicks powder
200ml whipping cream, chilled

Preheat the oven to 150°C. Line the base and sides of a 20cm square tin with greaseproof paper.

Combine the milk and vinegar in a measuring jug and leave to stand for 10 minutes. Once the milk has curdled, give it a stir, then whisk in the vanilla and eggs.

Combine the unsalted butter, vegetable oil, golden syrup, caster sugar and salt in a wide saucepan. Place over medium heat, stirring until the butter has melted and the mixture is on the verge of simmering.

Remove the pan from the heat and whisk in the egg-milk mixture, followed by the plain flour, baking powder and soda. Once smooth, scrape the batter into the lined tin and bake on a centre shelf for 45-55 minutes until risen and springy. Allow the cake to cool completely in its tin.

Meanwhile, make the frosting. Beat the cool butter and cream cheese in a free-standing electric mixer with a paddle attachment until thick, smooth and creamy. Beat in the icing sugar, followed by the condensed milk, vanilla extract and Horlicks. Whisk the chilled whipping cream in a bowl until stiff, then fold into the Horlicks mixture. Cover and refrigerate until needed.

Remove the cake from its tin to a serving plate, first freeing it of protective paper. Spread over the Horlicks cream, creating nice, swirly patterns.

COCONUT SPONGE

Although this tender sponge is best made with fresh coconut cream, liquid from a carton or tin should work, as long as it is has not been stabilised.

You can enjoy this cake plain, in all its fragrant simplicity, with tea or coffee. Alternatively, slather it with a cloud of whipped cream and carpet with fruit. A retro – and very jolly-looking – topping of cream, sliced tinned peaches and maraschino or glacé cherries is also recommended.

SERVES 8

180g plain flour
1 tsp baking powder
3 eggs
¼ tsp salt
175g caster sugar
125ml coconut cream (see above)
2 tbsp vegetable oil
2 tbsp water

Preheat the oven to 180°C. Line the base and sides of a 22cm square cake tin with greaseproof paper.

Sift the plain flour and baking powder into a bowl.

Beat the eggs with the salt in a freestanding mixer with a whisk attachment at medium-high speed until pale yellow and frothy. Gradually add the caster sugar and continue beating until the mixture grows even paler, turning mousse-like and leaving foamy but distinct trails when the beater is lifted. This should take 5-7 minutes.

Meanwhile, combine the coconut cream, vegetable oil and water in a small saucepan and warm over medium-low heat until just hand-hot. Do not let the mixture boil. Pour this coconut cream mixture into the aerated eggs, beating it in at a medium speed. Add the leavened flour in two installments, beating it in at a slow speed until uniform. (I usually do this manually with the detached whisk attachment; it grants the baker better control.)

Scrape the batter out into the lined tin. Smooth its surface and give it several sharp taps against the counter. Bake on a centre shelf in the preheated oven for 20-25 minutes or until pale gold and springy to the touch.

Allow the cake to cool for 5 minutes in its tin, then invert onto a wire rack, peel off the protective paper and leave to cool completely before treating as you so desire.

JAM ROLL

These were one of the treats I used to have in the canteen at the Julia Gabriel Speech and Drama Centre when it was at Halifax Road, alongside walnut brownies, raisin sponges, banana bread and fairy cakes, and packets of Capri-Sun.

SERVES 8

75g cake flour
1 tsp baking powder
4 large egg yolks
80g granulated sugar
45g vegetable oil
45g whipping cream
1 tsp vanilla extract
5 egg whites
Pinch of salt
6 tbsp good-quality raspberry jam
Icing sugar, for dusting

Preheat the oven to 200°C. Line the floor and sides of a 21 x 32cm Swiss roll tin with a large, overhanging sheet of greaseproof paper.

Sift the cake flour and baking powder into a bowl.

Place the egg yolks and 40g of the granulated sugar in a large mixing bowl and whisk until it thickens slightly, lightening in yellow by a shade. This only takes a couple of minutes by hand. Briskly whisk in the oil, whipping cream and vanilla extract, followed by the sifted leavened cake flour. The batter at this point should resemble a thick goo.

In a free-standing electric mixer, whisk the egg whites with a pinch of salt until frothy, then add the remaining 40g granulated sugar and continue whisking until stiff peaks form. Roughly stir a tablespoon of the whipped whites into the yolk batter to lighten it. Fold in the remaining whites in two batches until a uniform, well-aerated batter is produced. Scrape this into the prepared tin, rap it against the counter to remove any bubbles, then bake on the centre shelf for 12-15 minutes or until light gold and springy.

Drop the tray of cooked sponge onto your work surface from a 4cm height to expel any air pockets. Cool the cake in its tin for 15 minutes, then invert it onto a large sheet of greaseproof paper. With the help of the paper beneath it, gently roll the cake into a log, then unroll it: this makes it more pliable. Spread over the jam, leaving a 1cm border all around, then roll the cake up lengthwise, slowly but firmly. Smooth out its log-shaped body, twisting the excess bits of paper on either end to give it the appearance of a large, long candy.

Refrigerate the roll for 30 minutes. Unroll it gently onto a serving dish and dust with icing sugar.

MARCASOTES

Those of us in Singapore, Malaysia and Indonesia would recognise this as a variant of wheat-and-egg-based huat kueh or fatt koh, "prosperity cakes" in Hokkien and Cantonese, steamed, crack-topped sponges usually brought out during the Lunar New Year or as prayer offerings.

This recipe, however, is based on one of their kin that I encountered in Bicol, Philippines, as it was the first steamed egg sponge I attempted. Cooked into towering cylinders, this cake is known there as marcasotes, likely after marquesote, the sweet Mexican bread.

MAKES 3

200g Hong Kong flour
½ tsp baking powder
2 eggs
Pinch of salt
175g granulated sugar, for sprinkling
150ml carbonated water
1 tsp vanilla extract

Prepare a steamer. You require one with a perforated compartment that is at least 15cm tall. A trivet placed on the floor of a large wok containing a little water makes a decent alternative.

Sift the Hong Kong flour and baking powder into a bowl.

Line the bases of 3 x 6cm ramekins or dariole moulds with discs of greaseproof paper. Line their sides with collars of greaseproof paper approximately 12cm tall; they should dramatically rise above the moulds. (For improved security, I recommend fashioning said collars from wide strips of greaseproof paper folded onto themselves.)

Crack the eggs into the bowl of a freestanding mixer fitted with a whisk attachment. Add the salt and beat at medium-high speed until pale yellow. Sprinkle in the granulated sugar and continue whisking until mousse-like. You should be able to form trails on its almost white, cloud-like, surface. Add the flour-baking powder mixture in two installments, in alternation with the carbonated water, beating them in at a slow speed until uniform. (I usually do this manually with the detached whisk attachment; it grants the cook better control.) Finally incorporate the vanilla extract.

Divide the batter among the 3 moulds, give them each several sharp taps on the counter. Sprinkle a little granulated sugar over their faces in a criss-cross fashion.

Steam for 15-20 minutes until risen, cracked and cooked. An inserted skewer should emerge clean. Cool slightly before removing from their moulds and eating. (Or leave them on a wire rack to cool completely and then eat.)

ROCK BUNS

These are one of the first things I ever made with my mother: craggy-faced, scone-like beauties, fraught with dried fruit. They need no accompaniment, save cups of hot, milky tea.

MAKES 15-17

275g plain flour
A pinch of salt
2 tsp baking powder
135g cold butter, cubed
75g caster sugar
Grated zest of a lemon
175g mixed dried fruit
1 egg, lightly beaten
Approx. 3-4 tbsp milk

Preheat the oven to 200°C. Line a 20 x 30cm baking sheet with greaseproof paper.

Sift the plain flour, salt and baking powder into a large bowl. Add the cubes of cold butter and rub them into the flour to get a mess of pale yellow crumbs. Stir in the caster sugar, grated lemon zest and mixed dried fruit. Once evenly incorporated, stir in the beaten egg, then just enough milk to achieve a consistency between cookie dough and muffin batter.

Drop approx. 2 tbsp of the batter at 4cm intervals over the lined tray; these will expand, but not drastically. You should get 15-17.

Bake on the second highest shelf for 15-18 minutes or until golden and cooked through.

These are best eaten warm. They are decent cold, keeping well in a cool place but for not longer than two days.

DURIAN PUFFS

Read: profiteroles, slashed and stultified with durian cream.

MAKES 18-22

for the choux pastry
60g unsalted butter, cubed
¼ tsp salt
2 tsp caster sugar
125ml water
75g plain flour
1 tsp pure vanilla extract
Approx. 2 eggs, beaten

for the filling
400g durian flesh
175ml whipping cream, chilled

to serve
1 tbsp icing sugar

Preheat the oven to 200°C.

Place the butter, salt, caster sugar and water in a medium-sized saucepan. Place over medium heat, stirring so the butter forms an emulsion with the water. Once this mixture boils, beat in the plain flour until you get a thick paste, without any trace of white. Remove the pan from the heat.

Stir in the vanilla, then beat in just enough beaten egg to produce a smooth, glossy dough stiff enough for a spoon to stand upright in it. Let the dough cool slightly, then transfer it to a piping bag and make 2½cm discs on a large baking sheet at 5cm intervals. Expect to get 18-22. Any pointed tops may be smoothed out with lightly moistened digits.

Bake on a centre shelf for 20-25 minutes or until light gold. Remove them from the oven momentarily. Puncture each profiterole at the side with a fine skewer to relieve them of steam, then bake for another 10 minutes to crisp up slightly.

Transfer the profiteroles to a wire rack and let them cool completely. (They will deflate very slightly as this happens.)

Blend the durian to the desired consistency, then tip into a bowl. Beat the chilled whipping cream until it holds stiff peaks, then fold into the durian pulp.

Split the profiteroles horizontally, fill them with the durian cream either with a teaspoon or piping bag, then conceal them. Dust with icing sugar.

PINEAPPLE TARTS

These, for most Malaysians, Singaporeans and Indonesians, are the taste of the Lunar New Year. Known variously as kueh tair in Baba Malay, kuih tat nanas in Malay and kue nastar in Indonesian, they take several forms, from thick tiles to flaky baubles, latticed tarts to golden capsules. I fashion them after the starring fruit by branding their little bodies with harlequin score marks which, incidentally, helps camouflage any fissures that can arise during baking.

Broadly speaking, there are two ways to begin the pastry, by rubbing the fat into flour or whipping the fat with the sugar and then incorporating everything else. This recipe tots down the second path, the result light and delicate, as long as it has not been overworked. It has been spared condensed milk and milk powder, but has a little vanilla and some very untraditional grated parmesan, which delivers shortness and a delicious savoury depth to the crumb.

As for the filling, while most cooks would intimate a preference for grating the pineapples, making a jam fraught with lucent amber filaments, I take them to their maker in a food processor, not because it is easier, but for the chunky, deliciously irregular, texture it affords. As ever, you decide.

MAKES approx. 40

for the filling
1.4kg ripe pineapple flesh,
    peeled and cored weight
6 cloves
2 star anise
2 x 5cm cinnamon sticks
165g demerara sugar

for the pastry
220g unsalted butter, slightly
    softened
½ tsp vanilla extract
½ tsp salt
75g icing sugar
2 egg yolks
50g parmesan cheese, finely grated
270g cake flour
30g cornflour

Cut the pineapples into quarters and blend in a food processor until you get a nubbly purée, then tip into a wide, heavy-based, non-reactive saucepan. Add the whole spices and place over medium heat. Once it bubbles, reduce the heat and simmer, stirring to prevent catching, until the pulp has become a little translucent and most of the juices have been cooked off. A path created by your stirring implement should not fill up with liquid. Add the demerara sugar and continue simmering and stirring until a thick, dryish amber jam is obtained. The entire process should take 1-1½ hours. Decant into a bowl and cool completely.

Make the pastry: beat the unsalted butter with the vanilla extract and salt in a freestanding mixer at medium speed until pale and creamy. Add the icing sugar and continue beating until the mixture is fluffy. Drop in the egg yolks, one at a time, and beat until a light, moussey mixture is obtained. Stir in the grated parmesan, followed by the cake flour and cornflour, going in gently with your hands until a smooth, soft, paste-like dough, is formed. Cover and refrigerate overnight to firm up.

to finish
2 egg yolks, beaten with 1 tsp
   vegetable oil (egg wash)
40 cloves

The following day, remove the pastry and pineapple jam from the cold. Preheat the oven to 175°C.

Remove the whole spices from the pineapple jam and divide the tacky mixture into 40 balls, each worth about 1 heaped tsp. Arrange these on a tray. Do the same for the pastry; each ball should be 13g.

Prepare the egg wash.

Flatten a ball of pastry into a 4cm disc on a palm. Pop a ball of pineapple jam in its centre, then gently bring over the sides of the pastry, pinching its edges to conceal its cargo. Roll this first into a ball, then into a chubby oval. Place this on a greased baking sheet. Continue making all the tarts this way, arranging them smartly across the baking sheet, leaving a separation space of approx. 3cm.

Insert a clove into one end of each tart. Then, using a paring knife, brand their surfaces with criss-cross patterns and lightly paint them with the egg wash.

Bake the tarts on the second highest shelf for 17-20 minutes or until golden. If they have not attained the desired tan, hike up the heat to 250°C and watch them like a hawk. As they bake, their filling expands, producing cracks in their skins. As they cool, their filling contracts and the fissures appear less pronounced.

Cool the finished tarts on their baking sheet for 10 minutes, then carefully convey them with a palette knife to a wire rack. Let them cool completely before storing in airtight containers. This may be an unpopular opinion, but these seem better a day or so after they have been made, when jam and pastry have had some time to get friendly.

PUTERI AYU

One glimpse at the photo on the following page and it will be plain how these cakes earned their title; in Malay, puteri means "princess", ayu "beautiful". There is of course their form, dainty and crenellated, for which their moulds take full credit. While these come in various sizes, the ones employed here are 15ml in capacity. Mention must also be made of their two-toned, two-tiered bodies, their bases light green with pandan extract (not amphibian with E numbers) and crowns of coconut, which should be fresh and not desiccated.

Stabilising Ovalette is a common ingredient and probably essential if one is courting a large quantity that demands to be steamed in batches over a protracted period of time. Given this recipe's modest yield, I have left it out.

These make for a sumptuous dessert sullied with coconut sugar syrup, made by simmering 150g shaved coconut sugar (gula melaka), 100ml water and a knotted pandan leaf until slightly viscous, like runny honey. For something richer, add 75ml coconut cream and continue simmering until you arrive at something with the consistency of toffee sauce.

MAKES 30

for the crown
175g grated coconut
1 tsp cornflour
A pinch or so salt

for the sponge
60ml coconut cream
4 tbsp pandan extract (page 220)
100g cake flour
2 eggs
Pinch of salt
Pinch of cream of tartar
100g caster sugar
Vegetable oil, for lubrication

Prepare your steamer, filling its lower compartment with plenty of water. Lightly lubricate 30 x 15ml *puteri ayu* moulds with vegetable oil.

For the crown, combine the grated coconut, cornflour and salt in a bowl and mix well. Spoon 2 tsp of this snow into each lubricated mould, pressing down to compact it in. Divide these moulds between 2 steamer compartments.

Now for the sponge batter. Mix the coconut cream and pandan extract in a jug. Sift the cake flour.

In a free-standing electric mixer, whisk the eggs, salt and cream of tartar until pale, voluminous and mousse-like. Gradually add the caster sugar and continue whisking until it is almost thrice its original volume. Batter dripping from the lifted beater should leave loose trails.

Now, detach the whisk attachment and use it, as you would a regular whisk, to fold in the pandan-coconut liquid in 2 batches, in alternation with the sifted cake flour, until a smooth, pale green batter is obtained.

Divide the batter among the moulds, filling them to their brims. Fit the 2 loaded trays onto the steamer. Steam over medium-high heat for 5-7 minutes or until the sponges are springy.

Remove the trays from the steamer and unmould the cakes immediately. (The plastic nature of the moulds makes this easy work.) Arrange the *puteri ayu* on a wire rack or tray and cool slightly (or completely) before snaffling.

VIENNESE FINGERS

These can be enjoyed unadorned, dunked into cups of coffee or tea. Dipping their ends in melted dark chocolate just makes for something a notch more extravagant.

MAKES 28-32

225g plain flour
25g cornflour
½ tsp baking powder
½ tsp salt
175g unsalted butter, softened
125g icing sugar
Half an egg (30g), lightly beaten
½ tsp pure vanilla extract

for the chocolate icing
150g dark chocolate
1 tsp vegetable shortening

Preheat the oven to 180°C.

Combine the plain flour, cornflour, baking powder and salt in a bowl. Mix well.

Cream the butter and icing sugar until fluffy and pale yellow. Beat in the egg until well incorporated, then mix in the vanilla and the combined dry ingredients, until a thick, stiff batter is obtained.

Convey the batter to a piping bag fitted with a star-shaped nozzle. Pipe the batter into 4cm caterpillars on 2 baking sheets lined with greaseproof paper at 5cm intervals. Expect 28-32. Use water-moistened fingers to smoothen out any cracked edges if they bug you.

Bake on a centre shelf for 18-20 minutes, or until light gold. If your oven is not sufficiently commodious, then you may bake one tray at a time: this dough is fairly patient.

Leave the biscuits for 5 minutes on their tray, then remove them to a wire rack to cool down entirely.

Melt the chocolate with the vegetable shortening in a double boiler (or a microwave). Dip the ends of the cookies into the melted chocolate, shake off excess, then return them to their rack to set.

BAHULU

This Malay pastry is thought to have been derived from Portuguese sponge cakes, pão de ló.
Indeed, the list of ingredients and technique of the two are almost identical. It has resonance
with the Peranakan and Chinese communities in Singapore, Malaysia and Indonesia as well,
being a staple at the Lunar New Year coffee table.

Some recipes require the gentle frying of flour to expel excess moisture, producing an
airier, crisper bahulu. As this recipe omits this step, the result is tender and plush, qualities
preferred at the time of writing.

I use two bahulu moulds even though my oven can only accommodate one per
session, so as to avoid waste time cleaning and refilling. (If your oven is wider, good for you.)
The good news is that this batter can stand for 20 minutes or so without deflating.

The quantity of your harvest will depend hugely on the kind of bahulu moulds
used. If you are using standard ones with indentations designed to mimic cermai, Tahitian
gooseberries, then you should get 25–28. If you are using moulds featuring an array of shapes,
like fish and scallop shells, expect fewer.

MAKES 25-28

80g plain flour
10g cornflour
½ tsp baking powder
3 eggs, separated
90g granulated sugar
1 tbsp vegetable oil, plus more for
    lubricating
1 tbsp soda water
Salt

Preheat the oven to 210°C. Once hot, place one *bahulu* mould on a tray and feed it onto the second highest shelf to get hot. Place another *bahulu* mould on another tray and stick it on one of the lower shelves (its place is not important just yet.)

Sift the plain flour, cornflour and baking powder into a bowl.

In a free-standing electric mixer, whisk the egg yolks with 60g granulated sugar and a pinch of salt until mousse-thick and lemon-coloured. Whisk in the vegetable oil and soda water, then the dry ingredients in 2-3 installments until well combined.

In a separate bowl, whisk the egg whites with the remaining sugar and a pinch of salt until stiff peaks form. Gently fold this into the sugar-yolk-oil batter.

Withdraw the top tray bearing the *bahulu* mould and lightly oil the indentations before filling them up to the brim with batter. Return the tray to the same oven shelf – the second highest – and bake for 10-12 minutes or until golden and springy. Remove the tray from the oven, leave the cakes to sit in their mould for 7-10 minutes before fishing them out with a toothpick or metal skewer. This process is pretty satisfying.

While they rest, remove the other tray-borne mould you've left heating up in the oven. Lubricate, fill and bake as before.

Bahulu are best consumed on their day of birth, but you may store them in an airtight container in a cool place for 2-3 days.

PANG SUSI

This is a Eurasian delicacy and something of a forgotten treat, a soft bun enriched with crushed sweet potato, holding a cargo of spiced minced pork bejewelled with fragments of candied wintermelon.

As with most (if not all) traditional recipes, variations do exist. Some cooks add a significant amount of sweet potato to their dough, making it denser. Others add parsley and peas to their filling. Speaking of which, kindly avoid using lean pork mince. While there is little desirable about a greasy bun, a modicum of fat is needed for flavour and succulence.

MAKES 15-16

for the dough
200g orange-fleshed sweet potatoes,
    peeled weight, cut into 2cm chunks
300g plain flour
100g bread flour
75g caster sugar
½ tsp salt
2 tsp dry easy-blend yeast
100g unsalted butter, softened
2 egg yolks
2 tbsp lukewarm milk
2 tbsp water
1 tbsp brandy

for the filling
3 tbsp vegetable oil
2 yellow onions, peeled and chopped
2 garlic cloves, peeled and chopped
1½ tbsp ground coriander
1 tsp ground cinnamon
1 tsp five spice powder
½ tsp ground black pepper
350g pork mince (see above)
1 tbsp brandy
1 heaped tbsp fermented soy beans
    (*taucheo*), crushed into a paste
2 tsp light soy sauce
½ tsp dark soy sauce

Begin with the dough. Boil the sweet potatoes in a small saucepan of water until tender. Drain, put in a bowl, crush into a paste, then set aside to cool completely.

In a free-standing mixer fitted with a dough hook, combine the plain and bread flours, caster sugar, salt and dry easy-blend yeast. Let the mixer go at medium speed, just to combine them. Add the crushed sweet potatoes, softened unsalted butter, egg yolks, lukewarm milk, water and brandy. Once again, switch on the mixer, letting it whir at medium speed, until a smooth, soft and elastic dough is produced. This should take some time, about 7-10 minutes; the dough will seem slightly sticky at first, even a touch too damp. Have faith. Cover the bowl and leave it in a cool place for 2 hours, or until doubled in size.

Meanwhile, prepare the filling. Heat the vegetable oil in a large frying pan over medium heat. Add the onions and fry until translucent. Add the garlic, fry until fragrant, then add the ground coriander, cinnamon, five spice powder and black pepper. Cook for 1 minute to expel rawness, then add the pork mince. Cook until lightly browned, stirring to crush any lumps of meat.

Sprinkle in the brandy, and once the alcohol has burned off, stir in the fermented soy bean paste and light and dark soy sauces. Fry for a minute or so, until the fermented soy bean paste is fragrant, then pour in the chicken stock. Bring to a bubble, then lower the heat and simmer for 15 minutes, or until most of the liquid has evaporated.

200ml chicken stock (page 221)
60g candied wintermelon, chopped

for the egg wash
2 egg yolks, beaten with
    1 tbsp milk

Stir in the candied wintermelon, let it cook for a final minute, then remove from the heat. Allow to cool completely, then adjust seasoning with salt.

When the dough has risen enough, give it a punch-down to expel air, then briefly knead. Divide it into 40g portions and roll these into balls. You should get 15-16. Arrange these on a lightly floured work surface and cover with a lightly damp tea towel.

Lightly flour your hands. Flatten one ball of dough in one palm, then dollop 1 heaped tablespoon of the pork filling on its middle. Bring the sides of the dough over the filling, pinching them to form a sealed pouch. Lightly roll this pouch into a ball, then into an oval. Make all the buns this way and arrange them on 2 large, lightly buttered, baking sheets, at least 4cm from one another. Cover the buns with a damp tea towel and leave to proof for 30 minutes or until slightly puffy.

Meanwhile, preheat the oven to 180°C and make the egg wash.

Once the buns have risen slightly, bake them on the centre shelf for 25 minutes. (You may do this one at a time if your oven is not quite so commodious.) Remove them from the oven, paint with the egg wash, then bake for another 5 minutes or until golden and shiny. Leave to cool slightly before eating.

KINDNESS OF OTHERS

One of my favourite things about work as a food researcher is observing individuals preparing dishes they have known for much, if not all, of their lives. Getting to witness people perform tasks, at one with the rhythms of their kitchens, will never cease to be a treat. Being encouraged to participate in this dance, not to mention in the enjoyment of the result, is a real privilege.

As a child, I would often hover around our Philippine helpers as they slipped milkfish steaks into baths of vinegar, garlic and pepper and turned svelte eggplants over blue-lit burners. I would join them in the extracting of tamarind water for *sinigang* and the colouring of hot rice with sauce from an *adobo*. Over time, a panoply of Philippine dishes quietly wended their way into our family meals.

Indeed, many of my family's favourite dishes arrived from foreign sources, often unexpected ones. There is a dish of red-spiced, slow-cooked pork ribs, fragrant with leeks, that my mother learned from a childhood friend. There is the *sotong masak hitam*, squid simmered in its own ink with spices and aromatics, that a Malay neighbour used to send over the fence and later taught us how to make. There is the *ham cha* and a clutch of Hakka dishes that I used to have at the home of a former partner's family every Lunar New Year.

Their provenances notwithstanding, I consider the foods in this chapter kinsmen with others in this book, all jostling for a place on the roof of my mind at the mere mention of home.

SILKEN TOFU & SHABU-SHABU SAUCE

I first had this at a friend's home many moons ago. Her version was simpler, comprising silken tofu, shabu-shabu sauce and spring onions, eaten cold, not so much as part of a meal but a television snack.

    Silken tofu sold in cylinders, however inelegant and childish-looking, are ideal as they are often softer than their block-shaped counterparts. Also, shabu-shabu sauce from the bottle is recommended. Making your own just for this would be an admirable, albeit wasted, deed. As brands tend to vary in saltiness, taste and tweak as you see fit.

SERVES 2-4

for the sauce
150ml *shabu-shabu* sauce
3 tbsp *mirin*
5 tbsp water
½ tsp light brown sugar

to finish
250g silken tofu
2 spring onions, finely sliced
2 tbsp toasted sesame seeds
   (page 220)
Chilli oil, *optional*

Make the sauce by mixing the *shabu-shabu* sauce, *mirin*, water and light brown sugar together. Taste. Although balance is key, the blandess of the tofu means it should be a jot saltier than preferred.

Free the cylindrical body of the silken tofu from its casing and slice it into rounds. Arrange these in a shallow bowl (or bowls) in whatever way you prefer and pour over the sauce.

Zap over some chilli oil, if using, and finish it with finely sliced spring onions and toasted sesame seeds.

SARCIADONG SARDINAS

One of my mother's favourite lunches involves a tin of sardines in tomato sauce upended into a bowl and warmed in a loaded rice cooker. The fish would then be sprinkled with bird's eye chillies and calamansi lime juice. Here, the sardines succumb to sarciado, a Philippine way of cooking that involves introducing beaten eggs to a pan of fried fish simmering in tomato sauce, then gently scrambling them.

SERVES 2

2 tbsp vegetable oil
2 garlic cloves, peeled and
   finely chopped
2 medium red onions, peeled
   and cut into half-moons
1 tomato, deseeded and sliced
3 red bird's eye chillies, finely sliced
1 x 400g tin sardines in tomato sauce
1 tsp fish sauce
75ml water
2 eggs, lightly beaten
Salt, finely ground black pepper

to serve
Calamansi limes

Heat the vegetable oil in a medium-sized frying pan over medium-high heat. Add the garlic and fry until fragrant, then add the red onions and cook until they just begin to soften.

Add the tomato and red bird's eye chillies and cook for a minute. Tip in the contents of the tin of sardines, tomato sauce and all, fish sauce and water. Bring to a robust simmer, then reduce the heat slightly and simmer for 3-4 minutes, just so the fish pieces warm through.

Lightly beat the eggs in a bowl and pour them into the pan of fish. Count to 10, then gently stir, so that the eggs set into soft blossoms in the red sauce. Taste and adjust seasoning with salt and finely ground black pepper. Tip into a bowl and serve with calamansi limes and lots of rice.

CASSAVA UKOY

Generally, ukoy are deep-fried rafts of small prawns, frequently boosted with green papaya, sweet potato, spring onions or beansprouts, bound with a gauzy, annatto-tinted batter of ground rice and, at times, wheat flour. This version, especially popular in Western Visayas, Philippines, is prepared with grated cassava, more commonly referred to as tapioca in Singapore, and dispenses with the batter entirely. The replacement of annatto with fresh turmeric is a personal preference.

Some cooks add carrot to the mixture. I prefer it without, though sometimes stir in 25g chopped prawn flesh, which affords both succulence and sweetness.

Basimatsi is a seasoned vinegar from the Philippines, exhilarating and punchy. Its name is a portmanteau of bawang (garlic), sibuyas (shallots), kamatis (tomatoes) and sili (chilli). If you cannot get hold of it, just use regular coconut or cane vinegar instead.

MAKES 8-10

for the fritters
200g tapioca, peeled weight
1 garlic clove, peeled and minced
2 shallots, peeled and thinly sliced
1 spring onion, thinly sliced
2cm ginger, peeled and grated
2cm turmeric, peeled and grated
¼ tsp salt
Peanut oil, for frying

for the sauce
1 garlic clove, peeled and thinly sliced
2 green bird's eye chillies, thinly sliced
1½ tbsp *basimatsi* (see above)
1 tbsp calamansi lime juice
1 tbsp caster sugar
1 tsp fish sauce
Salt, pepper

Grate the tapioca on the medium side of a box grater – think coleslaw – into a bowl. Stir in the garlic, shallots, spring onions, ginger, turmeric and salt. It will look quite dry, with the ingredients only clumping when pressed. Shape between a pair of tablespoons into rough, egg-shaped cakes (or failed *quenelles*). Expect 8-10.

Heat 3cm peanut oil in a wide, deep saucepan over medium-high heat. Once hot, drop in the tapioca cakes and fry for 3-4 minutes until gold and crisp, turning them over midway.

Drain on kitchen towel and serve with the sauce which you make by simply stirring everything together.

ENSALADANG FILIPINO

Ensaladang Filipino is a salad of charred-then-flayed Chinese eggplants, salted duck eggs, tomatoes and semi-ripe mangoes. This version includes shallots and red bird's eye chillies and replaces the traditional accompaniment of ginisang bagoong alamang (fried fermented Acetes) with a light dressing of fish sauce and calamansi lime juice.

It is, in a way, an extension of the tomato and salted duck egg (nicknamed "red eggs" in the Philippines for how they are tinted magenta to distinguish them from regular duck eggs in markets) that I used to eat with fried milkfish and rice for after-school lunches. The conjunction of funk and freshness, powderiness and succulence, heat and saltiness, may prove alarming to some, but it gives me – and many Filipinos – great joy.

While the tomatoes should be flavourful and crisp, it is essential that they pack some acidity.

SERVES 2-4

3 medium Chinese eggplants, each
     approx. 75-90g
2 salted duck eggs
2 shallots, peeled and thinly sliced
2 red bird's eye chillies, finely sliced
2 medium red tomatoes, cut into
     fine dice
75g semi-ripe mango flesh, cut into
     fine dice

for the sauce
1 tbsp fish sauce
1 tsp demerara sugar
2 tbsp water
2 tsp calamansi lime juice
A little freshly ground black pepper

Puncture the Chinese eggplants in parts with a fork, then turn them over an appropriately sized burner until their skins are charred and they feel tender and squishy. Convey them to a plate, cool for a few minutes, then flay.

Rinse the salted duck eggs to remove their ash coatings, then boil them in a cosy saucepan of water. Retrieve and cool them beneath a running tap. As it is almost impossible to peel these without ending up with disfigured ovals, I cut them into quarters, carefully remove all fragments of shell, then finely dice. Place in a bowl and gently mix in the shallots, red bird's eye chillies, tomatoes and green mango.

Make the sauce by mixing the ingredients together. Taste and tweak the seasoning; it should be intensely savoury and mildly tart, with a peck of sweetness.

Make an incision down the lengths of the eggplants and butterfly them. Pile on the duck-egg-tomato mixture and spoon over the dressing. Serve with hot rice.

MONGGO GUISADO

This is much more than the sum of its parts, its drab appearance belying its complexities, the punch of the ginger and grassiness of the Indian horseradish against the sweetness of the pork and beans.

Flaked, deboned portions of smoked fish (tinapa) may be used in place of pork.

SERVES 4

125g mung beans
700ml water
1 tbsp vegetable oil
75g pork belly, cut into 2cm pieces
2 garlic cloves, peeled and crushed
1 medium red onion, peeled and sliced
4cm ginger, peeled and thinly slivered
1 tbsp fish sauce
¼ tsp freshly ground black pepper
1 bay leaf, *optional*
200ml chicken stock (page 221)
2 handfuls Indian horseradish leaves
Salt

Pick over the mung beans. Put them in a bowl, cover with water and soak for 4 hours.

Drain the mung beans and place them in a medium-sized saucepan with the 700ml water. Bring to a boil over high heat, then lower the heat, cover and simmer gently for 35-45 minutes or until a thick, loose-textured gruel is obtained, adding a touch more water if it needs it. (It will thicken into a mashed potato-like consistency upon cooling.)

Heat the vegetable oil in a large saucepan and warm it over medium-high heat. Add the pork belly and fry, stirring, until golden. Now add the garlic, red onion and ginger and fry until soft and fragrant, adopting some colour in the process. Add the cooked mung beans, fish sauce, black pepper, the bay leaf if you want it and the chicken stock. Bring to a bubble, then cover and simmer for 10 minutes. Its consistency should be thick but pourable.

Stir in the Indian horseradish leaves. Once these deepen in green and wilt, which should take a couple of minutes at most, the dish is done. Taste and adjust seasoning with salt.

PINAKBET TAGALOG

The pinakbet or pakbet from the Tagalog region of the Philippines is unlike those from the Ilocos, its provenance, in that it contains squash and foreign liquid, be it water or stock. Traditionally, it is the juices released from the vegetables, having steamed until shrunken and yielding in their banga (earthenware pot) that forms the sauce. The name pinakbet has its roots in pinakkebet, "to shrink".

In the Ilocos Region, they would often add bagnet, crunchy fried pork belly, to their pinakbet for texture and meaty savouriness. In its place, my yaya would use regular pork belly, cut into matchsticks, or leftover siu yuk, Cantonese roast pork, gleaned from a previous meal. And while pakbet in the Ilocos Region may be seasoned with either bagoong alamang (fermented Acetes) or bagoong na isda (a sauce of fermented fish, usually anchovy), it is usually made with the former in the south. It is hard to be precise about the amount of bagoong to use, as levels of salt and funk vary among brands. To adjust seasoning, use salt and fish sauce; the latter is especially useful if both umami and astringency are needed.

The cooking times stipulated are not set in stone, much depends on the vegetables – especially the squash. May good sense lead the way.

SERVES 4

1 tbsp vegetable oil
3 garlic cloves, peeled and crushed
1 medium red onion, peeled and sliced
3cm ginger, peeled and sliced
1½ tbsp fermented *Acetes*
    (*bagoong alamang*)
1 medium tomato, sliced into half-moons
100g Cantonese roast pork
    (*siu yuk*; page 207), cut into
    2x4cm chunks
100ml prawn stock (page 221)
175g kabocha squash, peeled weight,
    cut into 3cm chunks
75g yardlong beans, cut into 4cm
    sections
75g bittergourd, deseeded and
    sliced into 1cm pieces
75g Chinese eggplant, sliced into 1cm
    half-moons
75g okra, cut into 4cm sections on
    a bias
4 green finger chillies
Finely ground black pepper
Salt, fish sauce

Heat the vegetable oil in a deep saucepan over medium-high heat. Once hot, add the garlic, red onions and ginger and fry until fragrant and lightly coloured. Add the fermented *Acetes* and fry for 1 minute, or until it deepens in colour and loses its raw scent.

Add the tomatoes and roast pork. Cook for 2 minutes, stirring so the meat is well-coated. Season with a little black pepper.

Add the prawn stock, kabocha squash and yardlong beans. Simmer for 3 minutes. Add the bittergourd, Chinese eggplant, okra and green finger chillies. Cover and cook for 5-7 minutes, until the vegetables are tender, shaking the pan and occasionally (and gently) stirring to redistribute. If the vegetables have exuded an inordinate amount of liquid, uncover and simmer for a minute or so, just to reduce the sauce slightly.

Taste and adjust seasoning with salt and, only if you really must, fish sauce.

ADOBONG MANOK

Adobo is not so much a dish as a way of cooking, one that involves braising meat, fish or vegetables in an acidic liquid to varying degrees of dryness. This adobo features chicken, white cane vinegar and soy, brought to the Philippines by the Chinese, and is deep with garlic, black pepper and bay.

There is absolutely nothing wrong with adobo made over fire. Indeed, it is how most, if not all, Philippine cooks do it. But the charming thing about putting it in the oven is that the surfaces of the chicken pieces, especially their skins, develop a nice crust. Whereas a frying session towards the end of the chicken's simmering is required to achieve this, all you have to do here is arrange the pieces in a single layer in a snug ovenproof dish. Also, the sauce seems bolder, more sticky and intense.

SERVES 4

18 garlic cloves
4 large chicken legs, divided into thigh
  and drumstick
2 shallots peeled and sliced
3 bay leaves
2 tsp black peppercorns, lightly crushed
150ml chicken stock (page 221)
3 tbsp light soy sauce
1 tbsp dark soy sauce
150ml white cane vinegar
Vegetable oil, for frying

Preheat the oven to 190°C.

Peel 6 of the 18 garlic cloves and finely chop them. Leave the remaining 12 untouched.

Heat a generous amount of vegetable oil in a deep frying pan over medium heat. Once hot, add the 12 unpeeled garlic cloves and stir for a minute. Lower the heat and fry for another 5-7 minutes, or until aromatic and tender. Remove these with a slotted spoon to a suitably sized ovenproof dish (see above).

Decant all but 2 tbsp of the fat in the pan. Brown the chicken thighs and legs in it, in batches, then arrange these in the ovenproof dish, skin-side up.

Add the chopped garlic to the pan. Push them around over medium heat until fragrant, then add the shallots. Once these have softened, add the bay leaves, black peppercorns, chicken stock, light and dark soy sauces and vinegar. Allow the liquid to bubble viciously for 2-3 minutes to take the edge off the vinegar, then pour over the chicken and garlic in the ovenproof dish. Cover with foil and bake on the second highest shelf for 30 minutes.

Remove the foil and give it another 20 minutes, turning on the grill if the skins of the chicken pieces have not gone sufficiently crisp.

LAING

Now here is a dish for the jaded palate: dried taro leaves braised in coconut milk. It is a big personality, immensely savoury, rich and smoky. All you really need to go with is a mesa of hot rice.

You can find dried taro leaves in supermarkets easily these days. Try to get packets with leaves that appear robust and whole, not fine and broken. The latter takes hardly any time to cook and requires very little liquid, so what is meant to be a richly sauced tangle of beautifully textured greens may end up as a soupy, slippery-as-moss, mush. It will still be delicious, though.

In Bicol, where this comes from and is known by other names — laing is what it is called beyond its thresholds — they would sometimes use smoked fish and prawns in place of pork and even incorporate chunks of taro yam.

SERVES 6

2 tbsp vegetable oil
150g pork belly, cut into small chunks
2 medium red onion, peeled and thinly sliced
5 garlic cloves, peeled and finely chopped
5cm ginger, peeled and cut into thin slivers
1½ tbsp fermented Acetes (bagoong alamang)
1 tsp fish sauce
½ tsp caster sugar
50g dried taro leaves
400ml prawn stock (page 221)
300ml coconut cream
2 lemongrass stalks, tender portion only, bruised
4 green finger chillies

Heat the vegetable oil in a large saucepan over medium heat. Add the pork belly chunks and fry until golden and most of their fat has rendered down, about 8-10 minutes.

Add the red onions and fry until they have softened and browned in parts. Add the garlic and ginger and fry until they have released their aromas. Add the fermented *Acetes* and stir until it deepens in hue and aroma. Then add the fish sauce, caster sugar, dried taro leaves, prawn stock, coconut cream and lemongrass stalks. Bring to a boil, then cover, reduce the heat and simmer for 1¼-1½ hours or until the leaves are just tender. I recommend checking at the 1 hour-mark if the leaves need more stock or water.

Remove the lid and drop in the green finger chillies. Cook for another 15 minutes, or until the leaves are slippery and soft, the sauce, slightly oily from the split coconut cream. Taste and adjust seasoning with salt.

SINIGANG NA BAKA SA GABI

Sinigang is a soupy braise of meat, fish or seafood honed with some kind of sour or tangy element, most often a fruit, leaf or both. This may be señorita guavas, bilimbi, green mangoes, tomatoes, elephant apples, calamansi lime juice or, most commonly these days, tamarind pulp.

In Milkier Pigs & Violet Gold, I provided recipes for several sinigang, hosting pork belly and ribs, milkfish and prawns. Here, I offer one made with a combination of oxtails and beef shin, its broth silkily thickened with taro yams.

The traditional base for said broth is rice wash (hugas bigas) which, as its name suggests, is the water with which the rice meant to accompany the sinigang is rinsed. Instead of sending the cloudy water down the sink, you tip it into a jug, straining it to remove solid impurities if necessary. If the first wash seems a tad too opaque and musty, use the second or third. The liquid releases a scent of dewy tropical mornings as it bubbles and affords the finished dish with a refined silkiness.

SERVES 6

500g oxtail, cut into 3cm rounds
500g beef shin
2 litres rice wash (see above)
1 teaspoon black peppercorns
6 garlic cloves, peeled and crushed
2 tsp salt, plus more to taste
600g small taro yams, peeled
150g mooli radish, peeled and cut
    into ½cm slices
2 red onions, peeled and sliced
1 tomato, quartered
100ml tamarind water, plus more to
    taste (page 221)
3-4 tbsp fish sauce, plus more to taste
4 green finger chillies
100g water convolvulus, cut into
    4cm sections

Place the oxtails in a large saucepan and cover with water. Bring to a rolling boil over high heat for 5 minutes, then drain in a large colander in the sink. Rinse well to remove impurities.

Give the pot a good wipe, then return the oxtails to it. Add the beef shin, rice wash, black peppercorns, garlic and salt. Bring to a boil over high heat, then cover, turn the heat down to its lowest setting and simmer gently for 2-2½ hours, or until the meats are tender but not disintegrating.

Stir in the taro yams, cover and simmer until they are barely tender.

Drop in the mooli radish, red onions and tomato and cook for 7-9 minutes, or until the radish is translucent.

Add the tamarind water, fish sauce, green finger chillies and water convolvulus. Once the greens are tender-crisp, which should take just a few minutes, it is done.

Taste and adjust seasoning with salt, fish sauce and tamarind water.

CEREAL PRAWNS

A firm favourite at zi char and seafood restaurants, I learned to make this fairly recently from a close friend's mother.

Most recipes keep the prawns in their scuba gear. Much as this contributes to the overall fragrance of the dish, it puts a barrier between two of the dish's main components — the cereal and the prawn flesh — and can thus be quite the bugbear, unless the eater enjoys chomping on the shells, too. So I peel the prawns, only leaving their tails on, and coat them in an eggy batter that serves as an adhesive for the cereal, itself crisped and coppered in prawn oil made from the shells.

Milk powder is a common addition. I keep it optional.

SERVES 6

for the prawns
600g medium prawns
30g (½) egg, lightly beaten
25g cornflour
Salt, sugar

for the cereal
2 tbsp ghee
40 curry leaves
3 garlic cloves, peeled and minced
2 bird's eye chillies, finely sliced
125g Nestum cereal
1 tbsp light brown sugar
¼ tsp salt
¼ tsp white pepper
2 tbsp milk powder, *optional*
Peanut oil, for frying

Separate the heads and shells of the prawns from their bodies but leave their tails on. Devein the prawns and place them in a bowl with the egg, cornflour and a pinch of salt and sugar. Give them a gentle mix and set aside momentarily.

Heat 200ml peanut oil in a deep saucepan or wok over low heat. Once hot but not smoking, add the prawn shells and heads and fry until crisp and deep orange, about 7-9 minutes. Remove the shells from the pan and decant off all but 4 tbsp of prawn oil. You may keep the rest for future use.

Add the ghee to the pan of prawn oil and place over medium heat. Once foamy, add the curry leaves. When they sizzle, stir in the garlic and birds eye chillies and fry for a minute. Add the cereal and fry until light gold. Add the light brown sugar, salt, white pepper and milk powder if using and continue cooking until the cereal is golden and fragrant, stirring constantly. Turn off the heat for now.

Heat 2cm of peanut oil in a separate wide saucepan over medium-high heat. Deep-fry the prawns until they curl up and turn golden and convey them to a plate. Do not expect crispiness.

Quickly reheat the cereal mixture over medium flames, and once it begins to crackle, add the fried prawns and cook for a final 30 seconds just so the flavours can fuse.

OXTAIL STEW

We are talking big time comfort here. A duvet in edible form. Besides being wonderful on rice, this has great affinity with crusty chunks of bread, grilled, rubbed with garlic and drizzled with an olive oil so virid it stings. Extra virgin, of course.

SERVES 6-8

1½kg oxtail, cut into 4cm rounds
50g plain flour, for dusting
100ml vegetable oil, for browning
2 tbsp unsalted butter
2 large yellow onions, peeled and roughly chopped
6 garlic cloves, peeled and chopped
2 medium carrots, peeled and sliced
3 celery sticks, cut into 1cm dice
2 medium leeks, sliced
3 tbsp tomato paste
2 x 400g tinned whole tomatoes, drained
3 tbsp dry sherry
1 cinnamon stick
2 star anise
A pinch or so of ground clove
A little grated nutmeg
Leaves from 3 thyme sprigs
2 bay leaves
3 tbsp light soy sauce
1 tbsp dark soy sauce
2 tbsp Worcestershire sauce
700ml chicken stock (page 221)
2 medium red onions, peeled and quartered
2 large potatoes, peeled and quartered
3 tbsp crisp-fried shallots (page 220)
Salt, black pepper

Preheat your oven to 180°C.

In a large casserole dish or Dutch oven, heat the vegetable oil over medium-high heat. Lightly flour the oxtail pieces and brown them in batches in the hot fat. The goal here is not to cook them through but to develop a rich, calloused crust. Collect the browned meat in a large bowl and set them aside momentarily.

Discard the oil in the pot and give it a proper wipe-down with some kitchen towel; there tends to be a shocking amount of black matter.

Return the pot to the stove, this time over medium heat. Add the butter. Once that melts, add the onions and fry until slightly translucent and brown-edged, then introduce the garlic and fry for another minute or so, taking care not to burn them. Now add the carrot, celery and leeks and sweat them for 5 minutes.

Stir in the tomato paste, drained tinned tomatoes and dry sherry. Add the cinnamon stick, star anise, ground clove, nutmeg, thyme and bay leaves, light and dark soy sauces, Worchestershire sauce and chicken stock. Season generously with salt and black pepper. Once the liquid boils, clamp on the lid and transfer it to the preheated oven. Abandon it for 1¾-2 hours, or until the meat is just barely tender.

Gingerly withdraw the pot from the oven. Uncover, stir in the red onion and potato, then reinstate the lid and feed it back to the heat for another 45 minutes. By this point, both the potatoes and meat should be tender.

Serve sprinkled with crisp-fried shallots.

SOTONG MASAK HITAM

The version of this that I grew up eating bore sauce that was markedly thinner, almost soupy. Over the years, I have come to prefer it thick, so that it clings onto grains of rice more effectively.

In ideal world, your ink should come from sacs within the cephalopods. This recipe, written during an especially pessimistic hour, assumes that something will go awry and so uses ink from sachets.

SERVES 4-6

for the spice paste
3 garlic cloves, peeled
4 shallots, peeled
4 dried chillies, deseeded
2 red chillies, deseeded and sliced
2 birds eye chillies
10g ginger, peeled and sliced
1cm turmeric, peeled

to cook
600g medium squid
4 tbsp vegetable oil
1 lemongrass, bruised
1 tsp squid ink (see above)
125ml fish stock
¼ tsp salt, plus more to taste
¼ tsp caster sugar
4 makrut lime leaves, torn
2 tbsp tamarind water (page 221)
2 medium red onions, peeled and sliced
2 red chillies, thinly sliced on a diagonal

Make the spice paste by pounding the ingredients together with a pestle and mortar until fine and smooth. Alternatively, blitz them in a cosy blender, adding a tiny bit of water to help them along if necessary.

Prepare the squid. Tear off the wings and flay them. Tug out their heads, cut off the bit above the eyes and squeeze out their beaks. Cut the tentacles in two and the arms into 4cm sections. Slice the squid bodies into 1cm rings. Contain these various anatomical parts in a bowl.

Heat the oil in a wok or large frying pan over medium-high heat. Once hot, add the spice paste. Fry for a minute, stirring constantly. Reduce the heat to medium-low and continue frying until it is intense red and fragrant, having split in the hot oil.

Stir in the squid. Cook for several seconds, just until their surfaces are opaque, then add the lemongrass, squid ink, fish stock, salt and caster sugar. Bring to a bubble, then cover and simmer for 40-45 minutes or until tender. Add the makrut lime leaves and tamarind water and simmer without a lid for 5-7 minutes or until the sauce has thickened.

Stir in the sliced red onions and chillies. Once these soften slightly, pull the pan off the heat. Taste and adjust seasoning with salt.

CLAMS IN COCONUT MILK WITH SPICES

This is not a big-flavoured beast of a dish. Caught somewhere between gulai and curry, it is meant to be a gentle, chest-stroking number. The inspiration for it was a recipe for thisra, a golden Goan dish of clams, which I had picked up from a Madhur Jaffrey cookbook. I have taken it quite a distance from its template, which is more simply spiced and uses grated coconut, not its sweet milk.

In place of the slit green bird's eye chillies, you may use 1–2 sliced red chillies, which is precisely what I did for the photograph.

SERVES 4

for the spice paste
2 tsp cumin seeds
1 tbsp coriander seeds
2 tsp fennel seeds
4 cardamom pods
¼ tsp black peppercorns
3 garlic cloves, peeled
60g shallots, peeled
30g ginger, peeled and sliced

to cook
2 tbsp vegetable oil
2 medium red onions, peeled and cut
  into thin half-moons
15 curry leaves
1 tsp ground turmeric
1 tsp chilli powder
250ml coconut milk
4 green bird's eye chillies, slit
600g clams, picked over and cleaned
50ml coconut cream
1 tbsp tamarind water (page 221)
¼ tsp salt, plus more to taste
¼ tsp caster sugar

Dry roast the cumin, coriander and fennel seeds, cardamom pods and black peppercorns in a large, deep frying pan over medium heat. Once nutty and aromatic, tip into a pestle and mortar and cool slightly. Do not wash the pan just yet.

Once the spices have cooled, crush them into a fine powder. Add the garlic, shallots and ginger and thump those in, until a coarse paste is obtained.

In the recently used pan, heat the vegetable oil over medium heat. Once hot, add the coarse spice paste and fry until fragrant, about 4-5 minutes. Add red onions and cook until soft and translucent. Add the curry leaves, ground turmeric and chilli powder. Fry for a minute to remove their rawness, then stir in the coconut milk and green bird's eye chillies. Cover, reduce the heat, and simmer for 5 minutes.

Add the clams, cover and steam until they pop open, about 3-4 minutes.

Uncover, add the coconut cream, tamarind water, salt and caster sugar. Simmer for 30 final seconds. Taste and adjust seasoning.

ABACUS SEEDS 算盘子

Named for the way they are thought to resemble the seeds of a certain mathematical instrument, the only challenge one may face is the dough's insufficient pliability, resulting in cracks during shaping. If the mashed taro is properly hot when the tapioca starch is added, this should not be an issue. If for some reason your dough is lacking in pliability, flatten it into a thick patty, lightly moisten its surface, then heat it in a wide frying pan over medium–low heat briefly on both sides, just so its surface loses some opacity. Then convey the patty to a lightly oiled work surface and massage.

Dried cuttlefish, reduced to fine shreds, can – thankfully – be easily found in the dry section of most Asian markets.

SERVES 6

for the abacus seeds
200g taro yam, peeled weight, cut
    into 2cm cubes
90g tapioca starch
Pinch of salt

to cook
3 tbsp vegetable oil, plus more
    for lubrication
3 garlic cloves, peeled and finely
    chopped
15g dried shrimp, soaked and
    pounded (page 219)
15g dried cuttlefish shreds
    (see above)
50g dried shiitake, softened
    (page 219) and finely chopped
6 pieces dried black ear fungus, soaked
    and shredded (page 218)
75g pork mince
¼ tsp salt
1 tsp light soy sauce
75ml light chicken stock (page 221)
Pinch of finely ground white pepper

Bring a medium-sized saucepan of water to a boil over high heat. Add the taro yam and cook until tender, about 8-10 minutes. Turn off the heat, drain the pan of water and crush the yam directly in it with a potato masher. Total annihilation is the goal here.

While the taro mash is hot, sprinkle in the tapioca starch and salt and work everything into a smooth dough. You may use a wooden spoon, but I have asbestos hands. Leave the dough to cool.

Roll the cooled dough into marble-sized balls with hands lightly dusted with tapioca flour. Create an indentation in each one with your thumb to mimic corpuscles. Arrange these on a tray lightly dusted with tapioca flour.

Bring a large pot of water to a rolling boil over high heat. Cook the abacus seeds until they float and swell, almost doubling in size. Drain, rinse under a cold tap, tip them into a bowl and lightly lubricate with vegetable oil.

Now to the cooking: heat the vegetable oil in a wok or wide saucepan over medium heat. Once hot, add the garlic and fry until pale gold and fragrant. Add the dried shrimp, stir until aromatic and reddish, followed by the dried shredded cuttlefish. Once these pop and buckle, add the shiitake, black ear fungus and pork mince. Fry for 3-4 minutes so that the various components marry and meld, crushing

Light soy sauce
Red bird's eye chillies, finely sliced

the meat against the sides of the pan with your stirring implement to prevent clumping.

Stir in the salt and light soy sauce, followed by the cooked abacus seeds, chicken stock and white pepper. Once the abacus seeds have reheated, plumping up slightly, and the stock has mostly disappeared, about 3-4 minutes, your work is done.

Serve with small bowls bearing light soy sauce and sliced red bird's eye chillies.

HAM CHA PASTE

This recipe was furnished by a former partner, whose family used to invite me over every Lunar New Year to eat it with them. Ham cha, "salty tea", is the Hakka term for a dish more widely addressed as lei cha. The "lei" in the title does not mean thunder, as many assume, but the crushing action through which a paste of tea leaves, herbs, nuts, seeds, legumes and grains is made. This traditionally occurs under the influence of a wooden pestle in an earthenware basin with ridged interiors. As this requires elbow grease, it makes sense to make a large quantity, divide it into several batches and freeze them for future use. You could blitz everything in a cosy blender but I cannot promise it will taste or smell quite as extraordinary.

The tea leaf to use here is tieguanyin, 铁观音, literally "Iron Goddess of Mercy", a variety of Chinese oolong.

MAKES approx. 800g

150g mint leaves
140g coriander leaves
130g basil leaves
80g white sesame seeds
500g skinned peanuts
50g oolong tea leaves, such as
   tieguanyin
25g white peppercorns
Vegetable oil, for frying

In a wide frying pan over medium heat, warm 1 tbsp of vegetable oil. Fry the mint with a pinch of salt, just until the leaves wilt and deepen in green. Decant into a bowl. Cook the coriander and basil leaves separately in 1 tbsp of oil to similar effect, then add them to the cooked mint. The cooked leaves will release a notable amount of liquid as they sit.

Wash the frying pan and dry it thoroughly. Put it over medium-low heat. Once hot, toast the sesame seeds and peanuts separately until fragrant but hardly coloured; they should have just shed their rawness. Contain them in 2 separate bowls.

The pan's work is not done. Sprinkle in the oolong tea leaves and toast over medium-low heat until aromatic and brittle. Tip these leaves into a fresh bowl.

Sprinkle the white peppercorns into the pan and toast until fragrant and, again, tip them out into a fresh bowl.

Stream the greenish juices exuded by the cooked mint, coriander and basil into a measuring jug. You need approx. 125ml, but should get more. If you happen to have less, just top up with water.

Pound the cooked mint, coriander and basil with a large pestle and mortar into a mulch. Introduce the toasted tea leaves and crush them until they have broken down completely, melding with the pounded herbs. Add the white peppercorns and sesame seeds and do the same. Lastly, pound in the peanuts in several installments, adding 1-2 tbsp water if the mixture begins to look thirsty. Gradually add the 125ml reserved herb liquor, pounding until a fine, fibrous paste, like a dense, thick pesto, is obtained.

Divide among 2-3 containers (for ease of use) and freeze for up to 3 months.

HAM CHA 咸茶

The preparation of the individual components for ham cha may seem effortful, but none of it is difficult or time consuming.

Like many Hakka dishes, the result is not meant to be loud or emphatically flavoured, but delicate and nuanced. One of the bonuses of making this is the sense of virtuousness that arrives as you gaze down at a bowl exploding with green.

SERVES 6

for the rice
250g jasmine rice
2 tsp vegetable oil
2 garlic cloves, peeled and finely
  chopped
¼ tsp salt
375ml water

for the peanuts
150g skinned and halved peanuts,
  lightly toasted (page 220)

for the preserved radish
150g salted preserved radish
  (*chai poh*)

for the beancurd
1 tbsp vegetable oil
200g block firm beancurd (*tau kwa*),
  cut into 1½x½cm pieces

for the French beans
2 tsp vegetable oil
200g French beans, cut into 1cm
  sections
Pinch of salt

for the greens
2 tsp vegetable oil
2 garlic cloves, peeled and finely
  chopped
150g *kai lan*
150g *chye sim*

Begin with the rice. Wash the jasmine rice three times or until the water runs clear and drain well. Heat the 2 tsp vegetable oil in a frying pan and add the garlic. Once fragrant and lightly coloured, add the rice and salt and fry for 1 minute. Convey to a rice cooker, add the water and cook as you would regular rice.

While the rice is cooking, attend to the other components. Other than the peanuts, which you are to toast and contain in a bowl, and the obvious broth, everything else has to be stir-fried. Before proceeding, however, some (mildly annoying) prep work must be done. Wash the *chai poh* and soak in a bowl of water for 10 minutes, then drain and dry thoroughly. Cut the firm beancurd and French beans as described. Chop the garlic for the greens. Thinly slice the stalks of *kai lan* and *chye sim* and cut their leaves at ½cm intervals. Treat the sawtooth coriander as described. Pound the dried shrimp, cut the leeks.

This is where the instructions get repetitious, so bear with me.

Place a medium frying pan or wok over medium heat. Add the washed *chai poh* and dry-fry, stirring constantly, until they are fragrant and have swelled slightly, getting toasty in places. Convey to a small bowl.

Add the 1 tbsp vegetable oil to the frying pan and fry the *tau kwa* until pale gold, stirring gently to achieve an even tan. Transfer to a small bowl.

Wipe the pan and add the 2 tsp vegetable oil. Once hot, fry the French beans with a pinch of salt until tender crisp. Transfer to a bowl.

Pinch of salt
1 tbsp water
2 sawtooth coriander blades, thinly
    sliced

for the leeks
1 tbsp vegetable oil
25g dried shrimp, softened and
    lightly pounded (page 219)
300g Chinese leeks, thinly sliced
1 tbsp water
Pinch of salt

for the broth
2½ litres water
250g *ham cha* paste (page 195)
Salt, to taste

Now, the greens. Heat the 2 tsp vegetable oil in the frying pan. Once hot, fry the garlic until fragrant, then add the *kai lan* and *chye sim* with a pinch of salt and fry until tender crisp, sprinkling in the 1 tbsp of water for steam. Stir in the sawtooth coriander and transfer to a bowl.

Wipe the pan clean and add the 1 tbsp vegetable oil. Add the pounded dried shrimp. Fry until reddish and fragrant, then add the leeks, 1 tbsp water and a pinch of salt. Cook until the leeks have just softened. Transfer to a bowl.

For the broth, bring the 2½ litres water to a robust simmer in a large pot over medium heat. Lower the heat and stir in the *ham cha* paste. Once this has dissolved, turning the water a grassy green, lower the heat and simmer for just 2-3 minutes. Taste and season lightly with salt. (Some Hakka cooks do not add salt at all.) If you feel it needs more strength, add a dollop more *ham cha* paste.

Divide the rice and various embellishments among 6 large soup bowls and pour the hot, green broth over. Serve immediately.

ANG ZHAO ROU 紅糟肉

Producing the ang zhao, red rice wine lees, is not difficult, but takes time, and so only makes sense if you intend to use it regularly. Otherwise, outsourcing is the path to take, just make it a solid purchase.

There is no masking the fact that this emerges from the steamer looking like a car crash. I often finish it with finely slivered ginger which enhances the visuals and picks up on the husky notes in the dish. You may, of course, serve it as is.

SERVES 4-6

500g pork belly, cut into 2cm pieces
5 garlic cloves, peeled
25g ginger, peeled
5 tbsp vegetable oil
250g red rice wine lees
2 tbsp sweet yellow rice wine
   (see page 203)
1 tsp salt

Bring a medium saucepan of water to a boil. Add the pork belly pieces and blanch for 3 minutes. Drain and rinse the pieces under a running tap, then tip them into a bowl.

Prepare a steamer, filling its lower compartment with plenty of water and putting it over medium-high heat.

Crush the garlic and ginger with a pestle and mortar into a very rough paste.

Heat 2 tbsp of the vegetable oil in a deep frying pan over medium heat, then add the blanched pork. Turn them over in the hot fat until light gold, then convey them to a plate.

Pour in the remaining vegetable oil and add the crushed garlic and ginger. Fry them, stirring feverishly. Once fragrant and light gold, add the red rice wine lees and cook, stirring, until it deepens in hue and splits in the fat.

Add the sweet yellow rice wine and salt and return the pork to the pan. Give everything a stir and bubble for 2 minutes before conveying to a heatproof dish and steaming for 1¼-1½ hours, or until the meat is meltingly tender.

DRUNKEN OMELETTE 黄酒煮蛋

This is essentially a gingery omelette, sodden with hot, sweet yellow glutinous rice wine, 甜黄酒. What's not to like?

There are recipes that demand you pound the ginger, wring out its juice, fry the fibre in sesame oil and then reintroduce the juice. This recipe does not include this step, though you could: it seems to amplify the flavour and heat of the ginger in both omelette and broth.

As with the red wine rice lees, most Hakka make their own yellow glutinous rice wine. The process was highlighted in my previous book, Tamu, A Guest at the Bornean Table. Most of the time, however, I get it from benevolent friends and reliable shops.

SERVES 4

2 tbsp sesame oil
30g ginger, peeled and coarsely
  minced
2 eggs
A pinch or two of salt
600ml sweet yellow rice wine

Heat the sesame oil in a 22cm deep frying pan over medium heat. Once hot, add the ginger and fry until fragrant.

Lightly beat the eggs with the salt in a bowl and cast them into the pan. Swirl the mixture around to coat the pan and fry until a fluffy, softly-set disc with a crisp base is obtained, about 2 minutes. Break up the omelette into irregular sections, flip these over and cook them for another minute.

Pour in the sweet yellow rice wine and bring to a heady simmer. After 30 seconds, turn off the heat – you do not want to lose too much alcohol.

CHILLI-BRAISED PORK RIBS 辣椒排骨

This found its way into our home through my mom's childhood friend, Wong Pow Si, who is of Shanghainese descent. It is not, by her own admission, incredibly traditional, but is totally wonderful. Brands of dou ban jiang, fermented yellow bean chilli paste, can vary enormously in flavour and heat. The one to use here should be deep crimson with chilli but reticent with sugar. If yours happens to be insufficiently hot, add some chilli powder together with the leeks. If it is too sweet, omit the rock sugar or add a touch more black vinegar.

You could have this with steamed rice, but I prefer noodles, in particular those fleshy, gnarly, hand-shorn wheat ones from Taiwan.

SERVES 6

for the spice paste
8 garlic cloves, peeled
125g shallots, peeled
125g red chillies, sliced
25g ginger, peeled and sliced

to cook
100ml vegetable oil
2 Chinese leeks, white portions only,
   thinly sliced
2 tbsp light soy sauce
1 tbsp dark soy sauce
2 tbsp oyster sauce
3 tbsp fermented yellow bean
   chilli paste (*dou ban jiang*)
75ml Shaoxing rice wine
15g rock sugar
1 tbsp black vinegar
1¼ kg pork ribs, cut into 4cm sections
500ml chicken stock (page 221)

to serve
250g dried hand-sliced noodles
4 spring onions, finely sliced

Make the spice paste by pounding the garlic, shallots, red chillies and ginger in a pestle and mortar or blitzing them in a cosy blender, adding a tiny bit of water to help them along if necessary.

Heat the vegetable oil in a large saucepan over medium-high heat. Once hot, add the spice paste and fry for a minute, then lower the heat and continue frying until it is fragrant, deep red and has separated from the oil.

Add the leeks and fry just until they begin to soften. Then add the light and dark soy sauces, oyster sauce, fermented yellow bean chilli paste, Shaoxing rice wine, rock sugar and black vinegar. Fry for a minute, then add the pork ribs and fry for 2-3 minutes, turning them over in the spicy mixture.

Pour in the chicken stock, topping up with water to barely cover the ribs if necessary. Bring to a boil, then cover, reduce the heat and simmer gently for 1½-2 hours or until the ribs are tender and the sauce has thickened beneath a brow-raising layer of red oil. You may decant off the fat if you wish, but I tend to leave it in.

Boil the noodles in plenty of salted water, according to the packet's instructions, then drain well and mix into the red-braised ribs. Upend onto a plate and sprinkle with spring onions. You may use coriander instead, if you wish.

SIU YUK 烧肉

One of the key steps in making Cantonese roast pork is covering the pork belly's skin with fine perforations so that the fat beneath it can be released. There is a specific apparatus for the job resembling a torch light with metal spikes firing out of its head. Most people in the trade refer to it as a "poking device", which makes light of the damage it can cause. I have found it sold online as a meat tenderiser.

Take extra care not to be too vehement with the poking. If you penetrate the underlying layer of meat, juices will bubble up onto the skin and prevent it from blistering and crisping properly. If you have a butcher who is able to do this for you, so much the better. After poking, the pork has to be placed in the fridge overnight to dry out completely, then concealed in a robust layer of fine salt. There are cooks who recommend brushing the skin with vinegar, high-percentage alcohol or baking soda before salting. So far, I have been able to do the job without resorting to any of these.

SERVES 4-6

1kg pork belly slab
Fine sea salt

for the marinade
2 squares fermented tofu
2 garlic cloves, peeled and minced
1 tsp oyster sauce
½ tsp light soy sauce
¼ tsp salt
¼ tsp finely ground white pepper

Dry the pork belly on all sides with kitchen towel. Make small incisions all over its fleshy underside with a small knife. Crush the fermented tofu into a paste and mix in the garlic, oyster sauce, light soy sauce, salt and white pepper. Spread this on the underside of the pork belly, rubbing it into the incisions. Do not get any on the skin.

Place the belly on a shallow tray, skin side up. Pierce its skin multiple times with the poking apparatus, careful not to penetrate the meat. Give the skin a good wipe with kitchen towel. Refrigerate the pork overnight so the skin can dry out further.

Preheat the oven to 150°C. Remove the pork from the cold and let it come to room temperature.

Convey the meat to a large sheet of foil and wipe its skin a final time with kitchen towel. Bring up the sides of the foil to form a secure collar around the pork, rising 1½cm above it. Transfer to a roasting tray. Cover the pork with a 2-3mm layer of fine sea salt, firmly packing on the crystals and ensuring every bit of skin is concealed.

Roast the pork on the centre shelf for 75 minutes, by which time the salt would have formed a crust. Withdraw the tin from the oven. Increase the oven temperature to 240°C. Snip open the foil, pushing it down to expose the sides of the meat. Push the salt crust off the skin, letting it fall into pieces on the tray. Return the pork to the oven's centre shelf for 25-30 minutes, until the skin is puffy and golden.

NIAN GAO WITH COCONUT

I had initially thought of providing a recipe for nian gao. Then I realised that most of us will likely be plied with the stuff during the Lunar New Year and thought it may be more helpful to propose ways of tackling the glut.

Frying pieces into scorched, leathery rags is all very good, as is sandwiching them between wafers of squash and taro yam, battering and deep-frying. The ideas proposed here are different, resting more gently on the palate. The first, which involves steaming tiles of the stuff and tossing them in grated coconut, is popular in Malaysia and makes for a toothsome, fuss-free dessert.

SERVES 4

150g grated coconut
Pinch of salt
1 pandan blade, snipped
150g *nian gao*, cut into 1x2x4cm pieces
Vegetable oil, for greasing

Prepare a steamer and place it over high heat.

Place the grated coconut in a wide heatproof dish, mix in the salt and tuck in the pandan blade pieces. Steam for 5 minutes.

Meanwhile, lightly oil another wide heatproof dish. Arrange the *nian gao* over the dish at 1cm intervals.

Once the coconut is done, remove it from the steamer and lower in the plate of *nian gao*. Steam for 10-12 minutes or until the *nian gao* pieces have turned molten, edges blurring and almost bleeding into another.

Remove them from the steamer. With a couple of oiled spoons, convey the quaking *nian gao* to the steamed coconut and coat them well. Arrange on a serving platter and serve at once.

MUNG BEAN SOUP WITH NIAN GAO

This was something of a revelation, brought to our attention by one of my mom's former colleagues.

As the nian gao itself carries sweetness, the mung bean soup requires little sugar.

SERVES 4-6

150g mung beans
800ml water
½ tsp salt
1 tsp caster sugar
100g *nian gao*, cut into 1x1x2cm pieces

Pick over the mung beans, then wash and place them in a bowl. Cover generously with water and leave to soak for 4 hours.

Drain the mung beans, put them in a medium saucepan, pour over the water and bring to a boil over high heat. Reduce the heat, cover and simmer gently for 35-45 minutes or until the beans are tender, with some of their number melting into the soup, thickening it. You will have to give the pot a stir every now and then.

Season with salt and caster sugar, then drop in the sliced *nian gao*. Just as these begin to soften, their edges blurring and surfaces glossy, remove the pan from the stove and ladle into waiting bowls.

WALNUT CREAM 核桃糊

This, alongside almond cream, is one of my mother's favourite things to order at Cantonese restaurants.

While most recipes would instruct you to toast the walnuts in a dry frying pan or medium oven, I fry them in oil. This amplifies its nuttiness manifold, giving sumptuousness to the sweet, cocooning cream.

SERVES 4

4 tbsp vegetable oil
150g walnut halves
500ml water
20g rice flour
40g yellow rock sugar
1 tbsp light muscovado sugar
Pinch of salt

Heat the vegetable oil in a medium saucepan over medium heat. Sprinkle in the walnut halves. Reduce the heat to medium-low and fry them until deep gold. Take care not to burn them. Drain the walnuts and give the saucepan a solid wipe. (You may wash it if you prefer.)

Blend the walnuts in a liquidiser with the water and rice flour into a smooth emulsion. Pour this into the cleaned saucepan and heat it up over medium heat. Add the yellow rock sugar and light muscovado sugar, then half-cover. Turn the heat down to its lowest setting and simmer gently for 10 minutes, stirring to ensure it doesn't catch on the base of the pan. The finished soup should be shiny and silky. Add a little water if it has thickened too much. Season with a pinch or so of salt.

ES CAMPUR

In Indonesia, es campur is a sweet, iced cocktail comprising various fruits, sago pearls, nata de coco, cubes of agar-agar…the list goes on. This version borrows from a "fresh halo-halo" I learned of in the Ilocos, Philippines, made with locally grown melons, sweetcorn, avocado, jackfruit and sugar-cooked saba bananas.

It is sensational with fermented black glutinous rice (tape ketan hitam), though this must be made in advance. Wash 200g black glutinous rice, soak for 6-8 hours in plenty of water, then steam until very tender, sprinkling in 100ml water midway. Cool the rice completely, then massage in 10g finely crushed wine tablet. Store in an airtight jar and keep in a cool, dark place for 3-5 days.

SERVES 6

for the coconut milk
750ml coconut milk
100g caster sugar
¼ tsp salt
1 pandan blade, knotted

for the saba
75g caster sugar
250ml water
3 ripe saba bananas, peeled and cut
    into ½cm coins

to finish
60g small sago pearls
1 sweetcorn cob, husked
Flesh from 4 ripe jackfruit arils
    (approx. 60g)
300g ripe cantelope flesh
Flesh of 1 ripe avocado
Ice cubes, shaved or crushed ice

Gently warm the coconut milk with the caster sugar, salt and pandan blade in a saucepan over medium-low heat for 3-5 minutes, stirring to dissolve the sugar. Do not let it boil. Decant into a jug, cool it slightly and refrigerate.

Combine the caster sugar and water for the *saba* in a small saucepan. Bring to a boil over medium heat, stirring to dissolve the sugar. Lower the heat, add the *saba* pieces and simmer until slightly translucent and tender, with a waxy bite. Convey to a bowl and cool completely.

To a large pot of boiling water, add the sago pearls and cook until mostly transparent; the presence of tiny white cataracts are nothing to worry about. Drain in a sieve and wash under a running tap. Tip into a bowl and set aside.

Shave the sweetcorn kernels off their cobs. Slice the jackfruit flesh into strips. Cut both the canteloupe and avocado flesh into (vaguely) 2cm pieces.

Divide the cooked *saba*, boiled sago, jackfruit, canteloupe and avocado among 6 bowls. Pour over the chilled sweetened coconut milk. Add ice cubes or shaved ice and serve immediately.

KUMQUAT BRANDY

I first learned about this from a food magazine over a decade ago but only tasted it when my mother's friend, Lily Nah, gifted us with a bottle. A tiny glass is a fine way to wind down a meal, with or without dessert.

It would be remiss of me not to mention that slices of the butter cake on page 131 are sublime drenched in this elixir and eaten with cream. The amber liquid may even be used in place of the Shaoxing rice wine for the lor ark on page 115. Also, the drunken fruit can be chopped up and scattered over ice cream or stirred into cake batters, meat braises and Christmas stuffing.

MAKES approx. 750ml

500g kumquats
250g caster sugar
1 vanilla pod
2 star anise
5cm cinnamon stick
750ml brandy

Wash the kumquats and remove their stems. Dry the fruits well, pierce each one with a skewer or small knife and pile them into a 1½-litre sterilised Kilner jar (or something similar with an airtight lid).

Add the caster sugar, vanilla pod, star anise and cinnamon stick, then pour over the brandy. Give it a good shake to disperse its contents. Stow the jar in a dark, cool place for 2 months, shaking every other day for the first month, or until all the sugar has dissolved.

Strain the kumquat brandy into a clean bottle. Although the fruits have served their purpose and may be discarded, they still have some pleasures to offer, as adumbrated above. So please do consider reserving some (or all) and unlocking their culinary potential.

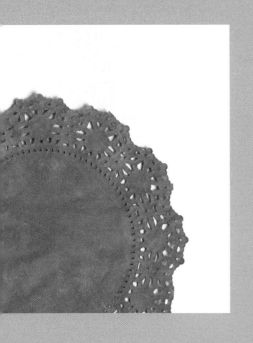

GLOSSARY

Alkaline water
This clear liquid is added to many Asian foods. It is responsible for the pleasant crunch in several wheat noodles and helps many sweetmeats properly set. It has to be used sparingly, however: go overboard and one will be met with biting soapiness.

Banana leaves
All over Southeast Asia, banana leaves are used to wrap many foods, from rice-based meals to pudding-like snacks. They generally need to be softened first, which can be done by running them briefly over a ring of flames until glossy and a more vivid green. Alternatively, they may be briefly immersed in a vessel of boiling water.

Beancurd sheets
This is made by cooking soy milk until a film forms on its surface. This film is then carefully removed and dried into sheets. They are either sold in this form or in an even drier state, with a generous amount of salt. The sheets I use belong to the latter camp and have to be de-salted before cooking, although it is true that low sodium versions do exist. To do this, wipe the sheets several times, thoroughly but gently, with a damp tea towel.

Calamansi
Also known as calamondin, *Citrus x microcarpa* is the most commonly used lime in Singapore and Malaysia. Its juice, both sharp and honeyed, is frequently squirted into salads, soups and drinks. A halved ball of calamansi commonly accompanies grilled or fried fish and meats, bowls of rice porridges and plates of noodles.

Chillies
The most widely used chillies in this book are cultivars of *Capsicum annuum*, smooth red or green fingers that grow up to 15cm in length and are mild in heat. These are also enlisted in their dried state, especially in spice pastes for braises. They usually require a brief immersion in boiling water to soften, first. Simply put the desired quantity in a bowl, deseed if necessary, then cover generously with freshly boiled water and leave for 10-15 minutes, until they swell and feel tender.

Also used in abundance is the fiery bird's eye chilli, *Capsicum frutescens*, the latter word meaning "bushy", referring to the stature of its plant.

Coconut
The grated flesh of mature (or nearly mature) *Cocos nucifera* may be added to *sambals* and used to frock sweetmeats, its cream and milk dolloped into curries and *gulai*. While one can get decent cartons and tins from supermarket shelves, nothing beats the stuff you wring out yourself.

COCONUT CREAM When the grated flesh of an adult coconut is wrung in muslin without water, one is rewarded with thick coconut milk, sometimes called coconut cream. 300g of grated coconut usually yields 125-150ml.

COCONUT MILK There are recipes that require coconut milk that has not been relieved of its thick cream. This can be achieved by pouring 250ml water over 300g grated coconut and squeezing the moistened filings in muslin. This yields approx. 300ml.

For recipes that need coconut cream and coconut milk separately, two steps are required. First squeeze 300g grated coconut with muslin, to extract the cream, as above. Then add 250ml tepid water to this once-used flesh and squeeze to obtain the second extract, the coconut milk. You should get 250-300ml.

Dried black ear fungus
Also known as rat's ear fungus or cloud fungus, specimens of *Auricularia polytricha* are commonly sold dried and require hydration. Put them in a bowl, cover with boiling water and watch them blossom dramatically; a little goes a long way. Drain, rinse under a running tap, incise out any tough portions, then proceed with the recipe.

Dried fish
In the Southeast Asian kitchen, several kinds of dried fish are used. In the context of this book, this means dried anchovies, dried cuttlefish (whole and shredded) and dried flounder, *tee poh* in Teochew, sometimes referred to as sole.

TOASTED DRIED SOLE Toast the desired quantity on the second highest shelf of an oven preheated 180°C, until golden and fragrant, about 10-15 minutes.

ANCHOVY STOCK Several kinds of dried anchovies may be used for stock. Large anchovies, or those about 2cm in length, often referred to as "Grade B" ones, must have their heads and innards removed as they can make the stock bitter. Place 50g in a bowl and rinse in several changes of water to remove surfeit salt. Put them in a large saucepan with 1½ litres water, 2 bruised garlic cloves and 2 thin slices of ginger. Bring to a boil over high heat, then lower the heat, cover and simmer for just 15 minutes. Strain.

Dried shiitake

These are useful for adding savouriness and meatiness to dishes. Soak the dried mushrooms in boiling water, cover and leave for 10-15 minutes, or until they have softened and swelled. Then, snip off their stalks and use their now spongy caps. Their bosky liquor is often used as well, and a recipe requiring this in a particular strength will specify the amount of boiling water to use. It is advisable to strain the liquor as the mushrooms may contain dirt and sand.

Dried shrimp

The shrimps are first cleaned and boiled in a saline solution until tender and orange. After getting drained, their heads are removed and their bodies are spread out on trays or winnowing baskets and left to sun until shrivelled, papery and crisp. Sometimes, the boiled shrimp are dried out on a large metal pan, gently heated from beneath by firewood. This hastens the drying process, turns their shells a deeper coral and imparts an appetizing aroma.

Once dry, a quick session of gentle abrasing helps loosen and free their bodies from their shells, which are then expelled with the help of moving air, either wind or an electric fan. Good-quality dried shrimp should be peachy to orange in colour and smell of the sea. They should not be musty or damp.

Dried shrimp normally require softening before being applied to dishes like salads or stir-fries or getting pounded into spice pastes. Soak them in a bowl of cold water for 5-7 minutes, then drain and dry. If one requires floss, pound them with a pestle and mortar or whizz in a cosy blender.

Eggs

Unless otherwise stated, the eggs used for the recipes in this book are large, 60-63g (with shell).

BOILED EGGS Bring a suitably sized saucepan of water to a boil over medium-high heat. Lower in the eggs (at room temperature) and boil for 6 minutes. Convey them to a bowl of cold water to stop them cooking, then peel under a running tap.

Fat

Vegetable, peanut and toasted sesame oils are the main oils used throughout this book. For deep-frying, I recommend peanut oil, which has a high smoking point.

Fermented black beans

These are not actually made with black beans but black soy beans. Fermented-then-salted, the resultant beads are wrinkly, gritty with salt, slightly soft in texture and pungent in both smell and taste. A little goes a long way.

Fermented shrimp paste

This pungent substance is known in Malay as *belacan*. It is made by sunning *Acetes* on winnowing baskets until half-parched, pounding them with salt to form a puce-grey mortar, shaping this mortar into bricks or patties, and then leaving them to ferment and dry out under a hot sun. A mere nugget is enough to transform any dish, be it a salad or braise, with its characteristic brand of fetidity and savouriness.

Before being applied to foods, *belacan* should be grilled or toasted. Ideally, this will involve pressing and wrapping the required amount in banana leaf, containing this in a grill frame and turning it over a lit burner. The goal is to get it dry, crumbly, scorched in parts and redolent of hot beaches. Most often, I wrap it in banana leaf and then stick it into a hot oven. If only a tiny amount is needed, like a tablespoon or so, I wrap it around a metal skewer and turn this over a ring of flames at the stove.

SAMBAL BELACAN Slice 125g red chillies, then pound with 2 bird's eye chillies, 1 tbsp grilled fermented shrimp paste (above) until smooth. Mix in 1 tsp sugar and 1½ tbsp calamansi lime juice. Taste and adjust seasoning.

Fish sauce

This is the clear, dark amber and saline liquid extracted from anchovies fermented in barrels with salt. While young fish sauce can be abrasively fishy, mature ones are more mellow and nuanced.

Garlic

Crisp, golden chips of garlic are often used to consummate soups, noodles and rice dishes. They may be bought from Asian grocers but are best home-made.

CRISP-FRIED GARLIC Finely chop 10 cloves of peeled garlic. Heat 2cm of vegetable oil in a medium saucepan over medium-low heat. Once hot, add the garlic and fry, stirring, until pale gold, and fragrant. Immediately tip the pan's contents into a sieve suspended over a bowl. Spread the chips over kitchen towel to cool and crisp up. If not using within the next couple of hours, these should be kept in an airtight container in the refrigerator, where they will last for a couple of weeks. The fragrant oil may be kept for other uses as well.

Honey dates

Also known in Chinese as *mi zao*, these crinkly, lightly frosted baubles are sweeter than regular red dates or jujubes; they are, in essence, their candied counterparts. They are often added to soups and drinks and are believed to possess medicinal properties, offering protection against the common cold and reducing allergies.

Noodles

Several kinds of fresh noodles are used throughout this book. To wit: yellow egg noodles; *mee tai bak*, "rat's tail" noodles, made from rice flour and tapioca starch; and *cu mi fen* or *laksa* noodles. (Avoid yellow egg noodles that reek of soap. Although they all contain lye, the best ones have a fragrance that does not scream out its presence.)

Dried noodles used here include rice vermicelli (*bee hoon*); beanthread noodles, made from mung bean starch (*tanghoon*); and knife-shaved wheat noodles.

Oyster sauce

This rich, chocolaty sauce is made of sugar, salt, oyster extracts and, for thickening, cornflour slurry. It is especially beloved by the Cantonese, though it is commonly applied to a wide gamut of Chinese dishes.

Pandan

Pandanus amaryllifolius is often regarded as the vanilla of Southeast Asia in the way it is used to add fragrance to foods. Unlike vanilla, however, pandan is commonly applied to both savoury and sweet items. Sometimes – and this is especially true for sweets – it is its rich extract that is needed.

PANDAN EXTRACT Snip 100g pandan blades into sections and blend with 400ml water into a fine mulch. Strain through muslin, squeezing to extract every last bit of juice, into a suitably sized jar. Seal and refrigerate for 16-24 hours, or until the liquid separates. The thick residue at the base of the vessel is what you use; you should obtain approx. 3-4 tbsp. A little goes a long way. This refrigerates well for 3-4 days, but is no fan of the freezer.

Those who seek a deeper hue but not the bitterness that comes with using more pandan may replace several blades with the scentless but intensely green *Dracaena angustifolia*, recognised in these parts as *daun suji*.

Peanuts

Roasted peanuts add richness, fragrance and texture to many foods.

ROASTED PEANUTS Spread the desired quantity in a single layer over a suitably sized baking tray. Bake on a centre shelf of an oven preheated to 170°C for 15-20 minutes, or until light gold and fragrant; they deepen in colour and crisp up as they cool. Although this technique applies to both skinned and unskinned nuts, the latter will require more discernment on your part. The best way to check is to remove one to a plate, cool it for a few seconds and have a bite. It will not be crisp yet, but should taste warming and rich, not raw.

Rice flours

The employment of different varieties of rice (what with varying levels of amylose and amylopectin) and processing techniques means that different brands of rice flour can produce disparate results.

Glutinous rice flour made from young grains requires far less water to cohere, forming a dough that usually cooks to a silky softness, whereas a powder made from mature grains will result in more bite and chew. Rice age, however, is hardly ever indicated on packets, so it helps to know which brand works for you.

Sesame

Both white and black sesame are used in this book. To toast them, sprinkle the desired amount in a wide frying pan over medium-low heat and push them around until fragrant. White ones will develop a pale shade of gold. For black sesame, you will have to rely on both smell and touch. They should feel light and brittle.

Shallots

These alliums form the foundation for many savoury dishes in this book. The ones I use are, roughly speaking, the size of large marbles. Fried shallots are often used to embellish dishes, providing texture, aroma and flavour.

CRISP-FRIED SHALLOTS Peel and thinly slice 10 pink shallots and spread them over a sheet of kitchen towel. Leave them for 30 minutes so that the excess moisture may be absorbed. Heat 2cm of vegetable oil in a wide, deep frying pan over medium-low heat. Once hot, add the shallots and fry, stirring, until pale gold and fragrant. Quickly retrieve them with a slotted spoon and spread them over more kitchen towel, where they will cool and crisp up. The oil that they would have infused may be reserved for future use.

Shaoxing rice wine
Slightly sweet, bearing with notes of marmite, this deep amber wine is made by fermenting rice, water and a small quantity of wheat. It is not interchangeable with clear rice cooking wine, which has a less complex flavour profile.

Soy sauce
Light soy sauce, brewed from fermented soy beans, roasted grains and *Aspergillus* moulds, is commonly applied to Chinese cooking for seasoning, affording saltiness, aroma, nuance and umami. Dark soy sauce boasts a higher salt content, though this is made less obvious by the addition of sugar. It tends to be used more for colour than flavour.

Stocks
The recipes in this book uses stocks made from anchovy (page 218), chicken, pork and prawn.

CHICKEN STOCK Place 1x1.2-1.4kg chicken in a pot and cover with 2 litres water. Drop in a garlic clove, 2 spring onions, 1 teaspoon salt and a tiny lump of rock sugar. Bring to a boil for 2 minutes, then lower the heat, cover and simmer for 2 hours. Strain the liquid. For greater clarity, cool and refrigerate it, then skim off the fat which would have neatly solidified on its surface.

PORK STOCK Place 1.5kg pork ribs in a pot of boiling water. Boil for 5-7 minutes, then drain and wash the ribs. Put these in a fresh pot, then add 2 litres water, 2 garlic cloves, 4 spring onions, 10 white peppercorns, 1 teaspoon salt and a tiny lump of rock sugar. Bring to a boil for 2 minutes, then lower the heat, cover and simmer for 2 hours. Strain the stock. For greater clarity, cool and refrigerate it, then skim off the fat which would have solidified on its surface.

PRAWN STOCK Heat 1 tbsp vegetable oil in a large saucepan over medium heat. Add 1 bruised unpeeled garlic clove, 2cm crushed ginger and 500g prawn heads and shells. Reduce the heat slightly and fry, stirring, until the heads and shells are deep orange and fragrant. Careful not to burn them; this will make the stock acrid. Add 1 litre water, bring to a boil, then lower the heat, half-cover and simmer for 30 minutes. Strain, crushing every last bit of goodness from the sieve or colander.

Sugar
Besides the white and icing sugars with which everyone is familiar, rock sugar and a variety of palm sugars, in this case coconut, are also commonly used in dishes both sweet and savoury.

ROCK SUGAR Produced by cooling sugar syrup into crystals, rock sugar is not as sharply saccharine as regular caster. It can also add a fetching gloss to sauces. There are 2 main kinds of rock sugar, yellow and white, sold in either irregular chunks or smooth, opalescent lumps.

COCONUT SUGAR This is widely known in Malaysia and Singapore as *gula melaka*. It is important to remember that flavour, aroma and sweetness can differ among batches. A rich, floral and almost toffee-like fragrance, and a faint stickiness, are desirable traits. Those that are rock hard and mutely fragrant have likely been corrupted with caster sugar. They are more suited to self-defense than the kitchen.

Depending on the manufacturer, *gula melaka* may contain traces of undesirable materials, like pebbles and basket fibre, and are thus best diluted in water and strained. When a mere lump is required for a dish, however, I usually just crush it between my fingers or chop it with a knife and add it straight to the pot.

Sweet flour sauce
A smooth, almost treacly, dark sauce made from fermented wheat flour. It is usually sought out as a condiment but may be used in dishes as well.

Tamarind
Pulp from the fruit pods of *Tamarindus indica* is a common souring agent throughout Southeast Asia. Tamarind water may be derived from store-bought blocks of this ripened pulp, usually sold in packets fraught with seeds. These vary in colour, from umber to deep mahogany, and should feel moist and heavy, the last an indication of substance.

TAMARIND WATER Dissolve 40g tamarind pulp in 125ml boiling water, then strain. This should produce approx. 125ml.

INDEX

Acknowledgements

None of this would have been possible with the support of my mother, Ginny, and sister, Dawn. My gratitude is extended to Zeng Zhiyong, for sharing with me his family's Hakka recipes and whose beautiful paper ixoras rest on the front cover; Tan Aye Leng, who helped me with the Teochew chapter; Wong Pow Si, for her chilli pork rib recipe; and my *yayas* who fed and humoured me.

Also, heartfelt thanks to my editor Meena Mylvaganam; Dylan Lau, for his keen eye; and Wilson Wang of Papier Blanc for his exquisite endpapers.

THE AUTHOR

Bryan Koh is an award-winning author of four cookbooks. His breakthrough, *Milk Pigs & Violet Gold* (2014), won the Best Food Book Award at the Philippine National Book Awards. Its second edition *Milkier Pigs & Violet Gold* was released in 2020.

His second book, *Mornings are for Mohinga, Burmese Food Stories* (2015), won third place in the Best Asian Cookbook category at the World Gourmand Cookbook Awards 2016. His third book, *Bekwoh* (2018) focused on the food of East Coast Peninsular Malaysia, his fourth, *Tamu*, on the food of Borneo.

Bryan majored in Mathematics at the National University of Singapore and has a Masters in Management Hospitality from Cornell University. He lives in Singapore and is co-owner of cake company Chalk Farm.

Other releases

MILKIER PIGS & VIOLET GOLD
Philippine Food Stories

MORNINGS ARE FOR MOHINGA
Burmese Food Stories

BEKWOH
Stories & Recipes from Peninsular Malaysia's East Coast

TAMU
A Guest at the Bornean Table

Published by Xochipilli

ISBN: 978-981-18-6361-5
Editor: Meena Mylvaganam
Art Direction, Design and Layout: Bryan Koh

Name(s): Koh , Bryan.
Title: Among ixoras : a collection of recipes from my
kitchen in Singapore / Bryan Koh.
Description: [Singapore] : Xochipilli, [2023]
Identifier(s): ISBN 978-981-18-6361-5 (hardback)
Subject(s): LCSH: Cooking, Singaporean.
Classification: DDC 641.595957 --dc23

Studio photographs © 2023 Bryan Koh
Author photograph © 2023 Darren Gabriel Leow
Endpapers © 2023 Papier Blanc

Printed in Singapore